MAGICAL ENCOUNTERS

By
Busta Akong
Constant Madon Ph.D

WIPF & STOCK · Eugene, Oregon

Wipf and Stock Publishers
199 W 8th Ave, Suite 3
Eugene, OR 97401

Magical Encounters
By Madon, Constant and Akong, Busta
Copyright©2010 by Madon, Constant
ISBN 13: 978-1-5326-6361-1
Publication date 7/24/2018
Previously published by PublishAmerica, 2010

Table of Contents

INTRODUCTION 7
PROLOGUE 11

Bob's Stories

THE JAIL 15
MY YOUTH 17
MY SKATES AND SKATING 21
HOW ONE MAN CHANGED MY LIFE 26
MY WIFE 28
THE MILITARY 30
LIVING IN THE SOUTH IN THE 60'S 39
JACK, BOBBY, MARTIN-THE 60'S 41
WALL STREET 42
ON MEETING LILY 47
COMING HOME 50
MY ENERGY WORK 56
ALICE BROWN 70

Jim's Stories

MY FATHER 89
THE SEARCH PARTY 90
RIDING THROUGH THE COCOANUT FARM 92
SPIRIT TAKES OVER 93
MY FISHING TRIPS 94
SATURDAY NIGHT DANCE 95

MY OPERATION	96
HAPPY TIMES/SAD TIMES	98
THREE DAYS LATER	101
HOW MY CAR WAS MADE NEW AGAIN-SPIRIT DOES IT	103
MY SECOND OPERATION	106
I HAD A DREAM	108
MY WONDERFUL SON AND DAUGHTER	109
A SPECIAL FRIEND	111
MY MOM PASSED AWAY AND IS IN SPIRIT	113
MY FRIEND IS NOW IN SPIRIT	116
HOW I CAME TO BE HERE AT THE CENTER	118
THREE NEAR COLLISIONS-HOW SPIRIT GUIDES ME	120
MY TRIP TO TORONTO-SPIRIT TOOK OVER	123
THE LOTTERY	125
I NEEDED MONEY-SPIRIT PROVIDED IT	128
MY ASTRAL DREAMS	129
THAT BUS NEARLY HIT ME	135
HOW MY LANDLORD GOT POORER	137
THE LADY AND HER FEATHER	139
THE POWER CIRCLE	141
A JOURNEY INTO THE RAIN FOREST	143
EPILOGUE	147

INTRODUCTION

What is this book about and why is it worth reading?

This book is about the lives of two men, on a journey to spiritual awareness.

All of the stories are true. The life of each person unfolds in unusual and magical ways. None of the snippets are accidental. Each is there for a purpose. Each is there to show that though their journey is unique, the end goal of each is of the spirit, and not of the material world around them.

The world they now see is invisible, yet very real. It is the place they yearn to be, the place wherever it may be, is where they are supposed to be.

Some of the lessons learned are painful others are exceedingly joyful. They paint an invisible path from the material to the spiritual.

Now we turn to the main characters, Bob and Jim.

Would you like to look into our hearts and see who we are? Yes.

Well, this is what we have done. We have told stories, stories, which allow you to see and understand who we are. Our stories are from special memories that are locked in our hearts and remain there except for the telling. We believe that the stories we hold in our hearts tell who we are. Sometimes an instant, a moment can define and change a person's life forever. We've done this with our stories.

Bob Waters was born in a small town in upstate New York. He shares with you his childhood memories and relates to you one very important moment in high school that changed his life forever. Late in his career he found peace with a second defining moment, one that brought him to the top of the heap. Yet between these events, he felt something was missing. It was only in retirement that he found his true path, one that led him to peace and tranquility. However, it was not without a painful experience that changed him forever.

Jim was born in Trinidad, the youngest of eight children. His parents and grandparents had a long tradition of living their lives in Spirit. Jim learned about his gift at the early age of six or seven and his ability to see events before they happen. He is a clairvoyant. His stories are in sharp contrast with Bob's. Jim has lived in Spirit throughout his life. He lives a mystical life guided by his Spirits and Angels. They tell him many things, things that he has used to help and guide people and make their lives better. Jim's mystical experiences include astral travel with many of his stories telling about his astral journeys. Jim's spiritual experiences guided him to the Center in Montreal, Canada, where he now teaches.

In mid August of 2007, Bob while teaching at the Center met Jim. Bob related to Jim that he was having a personal crisis in his life and asked Jim for his help. Jim, using his clairvoyant powers, did a reading for him. The reading foretold the outcome of Bob's problem.

Later in the day they talked again and Bob said, "Why don't we write a book and tell our stores." And that's how it all began. We exchanged stories over the next few months and now we want to share them with you.

You are probably wondering why we did this. Let me explain. First, we wanted you to see and understand who we are. We felt the best way of doing this would be by telling stories from defining moments in our lives. Second, we want to encourage you to do the same, for your stories are your own personal biography. By telling stories that are etched in your heart, you will reveal to everyone, your family and friends, the true you. This is why we have left a few blank pages at the end of this book so you can get started.

We have changed our names and the names of the characters in the book.

PROLOGUE

The stories we tell, define who we are. In this book we tell our stories and the stories passed down to us from our parents and grandparents. There is magic in telling stories. The great teacher, Jesus, told stories that have been passed down for thousands of years. It is from these stories that we come to understand who Jesus was. So, too, it is with our stories that we reveal who we are. We take you on a journey, two separate journeys in fact that capture the magic in our lives, our inner hopes and dreams, the stuff that makes us get up each day and renew this hope, that each new day holds a promise of something better. Some of our stories are real, some are mystical, some require a simple yes and some require a faith beyond that which is real, some are humorous, others are poignant, some come from the joy of youth and some tell the heartache of reality, yet in the overall they tell who we truly are.

BOB'S STORIES

THE JAIL

My name is Bob. I was arrested, brought to the local State Trooper barracks, fingerprinted, photographed and booked. I was then escorted to the Town Jail, a large sprawling, modern, facility. My civilian clothes were tagged and I was given an orange prison uniform.

The guard said, "Walk on the right side of the hallway. You must always walk on the right side of the hallway."

I did as he said. I was escorted down two or three long hallways deep into the heart of the prison to a cell. I was in a lock down cell, in solitary confinement. The cell was about 8 feet by 10 feet with a toilet and sink, all made of stainless steel and a stainless steel cup. The full-length door was made of plexus glass and everyone from across the room could see into the cell. I had no toothpaste, no razor, no comb and only liquid soap from a push button spigot. My cot had a sheet and a blanket. The lights were bright and always stayed on day and night. The only way to sleep was to place the blanket over my head. There was no clock, so I never knew what time it was. There was a window about 3 feet long and 4-6 inches wide, just barely enough opening to let some light in. There was a small shelf with a half roll of toilet paper and a 4-inch toothbrush. There was a head count several times a day. You had to request a shower and a razor the night before. The shower had no soap and you were given a towel and then had to give it back. The guard watched while you used the razor and then took it back after I had finished shaving. I had to wait at least two days for a shower and a razor and the guard said I was lucky to get them.

At age 72, the shock to my psyche was devastating. I had never had any dealings with law enforcement except for minor traffic tickets.

MY YOUTH

I lived in a small city in upstate New York with a population of about 19,000. Since my parents had no car my only means of transportation was walking or riding my bicycle. We lived in the newly developed part of town on the south side of the city. It was a wooded area with few houses on the street. I, and my friends would often gather, on two streets and play 'kick the can' or cops and robbers. Summers we would play baseball in an empty lot.

I was about age 11 or 12 at the time, the youngest member of the team. The other boys were in their teens and much larger than me. They said that I couldn't play because I was too young. They had a ritual that they followed each day on how to set up the teams. Two players would volunteer as Captains. They started by tossing the bat, to each other then grabbing it hand over hand alternating back and forth. The one who got to the top of the bat first chose the first player. Then they alternated back and forth choosing the players for their team. Since the Capitan of each team was not the same everyday, and was the one to pick his team players, the team makeup varied each day. The infield was always chosen first among the team players. Since there were no assigned positions you got a chance to play different positions each day depending on the makeup of the team. Sometimes one team had an extra player and he would play the outfield and that team had four players in the outfield instead of three. Or on other days we were short players and there were only two players in the outfield. None of this really mattered, what really mattered was that we were to play ball. One day we were short a player and finally I got a chance to play the game. At that moment I felt that I grew three inches taller. From that day on I stood in the group with the older boys waiting to be chosen. I remember 'gee', I wish I was older so I could hit the ball harder and play the game better.'

We were really a group of rag tag players. Not all of the players had mitts. Those who didn't usually had to play the outfield. I often wondered what it was like trying to snag a fly ball out of the air with your bare hands. I was thinking, 'that must really sting like hell.' I got a lucky break one day when one of my cousins gave me a first baseman's mitt. It was a regulation size mitt, not a child's. When I first put it on it seemed huge but it made me feel older and now I really fit in. Next to my skates, that mitt was my next most prized possession. The mitt had a long pocket in which to catch the ball the pocket also helped to take some of the sting out when catching a fast ground ball. I liked playing first base because there was always plenty of action. Next to the pitcher and catcher, the fist baseman is always busy. Unless there is fly ball to the outfield, there usually is a throw to first. I remember standing in the infield trying to imagine what the batter would do. Would he strike out or hit a ground ball or a fly ball? Would he hit it to me or someone else? I was always focusing on the game and being in the moment shutting out everything else. That was the wonderful part of the game.

We played in a sand lot. There were no bases, just round sand indentations where the bases should be. That left a lot to wiggle room when it came to deciding if a player was safe or out. There was no umpire so the players would decide the close calls between both sides. There never were any real arguments like you see today in sports. We respected each other and gave each other the 'benefit of the doubt' in those close calls. There were no batting ranges like we have today where you could practice your hitting skills. I was never really good at hitting the ball when it was my turn at bat, but I did get pretty good playing first baseman. It always seemed to me that the pitcher was bigger and stronger and threw the ball harder. That scared me a bit and prevented me from fully focusing on the game the way I should have.

We often played until sunset before calling it quits for the day. Whatever the score was, it was. It never really mattered. We played, not for the score but for the fun of playing the game. We all got pretty dirty playing in that sand lot. I would go home with sand all over me and would have to 'brush down' before going into the house and then take a bath.

I became friends with a player who lived on the next street and we would play pitch and catch for hours on end. He wanted to be a pitcher so he would practice his fastball. At first I had trouble catching his fastballs but then I got used to it. Some of them stung real hard even though I had my big first baseman's mitt. Then we would practice throwing ground balls and scooping them up. This practice really helped me when I was playing first base on the team. So, I was playing baseball.

Of course I didn't realize it then, we never do, that they were the best, most carefree days of my life. It's funny when you are young you wish that you were older and when you are older you wish that you were young again. You yearn for those simple times, like playing ball in an empty lot.

It all seemed so easy then. Now I find that I have to make a conscious effort not to allow myself to drift back to the past or worrying about what tomorrow will bring. I try to stay centered in the now.

MY SKATES AND SKATING

At about age 11 or 12 during summer vacation I started to caddy at the local golf course, which was about 10 miles from my home. I remember the first day. I walked down my street to the main highway where I was going to hitch hike. When I got there another boy was already standing there also hitchhiking.

He said, "You can't stand here. Go to the end of the line" which meant that I had to go down the road and stand farthest away from the oncoming cars. That's how we took turns getting a ride. When I got there, I had to walk about a quarter mile to the field house. Once there we all sat on a log about a foot in diameter.

Pete, the Caddy Master, was a big strapping man. He would come out and point his finger and say, " I want two or I want four." It meant that two or four of us would go to the first tee and pick up our bags. We took turns on that log. It was an honor system and it worked quite well. If someone jumped up out of turn and took someone's 'loop' as we called it, they were not allowed come back the next day. If they didn't follow these rules they got beat up quite badly by the other boys. We got 50 cents per bag. When there were not enough caddies and we carried two bags and made $1.00 plus tips. On a good day with two 'doubles' or two bags morning and afternoon, we could make anywhere from $2.00 to $4.00. To me that was big money. From the day after school ended in June until it started again in September, if possible, I caddied 7 days a week.

One year I saved all my money and bought a new pair of Planert speed skates. They were the best ones made at the time. You measure each foot and send the measurements to the company in Chicago. They custom made the shoes of the skates to fit your feet. Then they sent the shoes back to you for fit. If any changes were needed they would correct the shoe and then attached the blades and returned the skates to you. They cost about $50.00, but they were the best money could buy. The shoes were made of kangaroo hide and the blades were made of special tempered steel. After 60 years this is the only treasure that I have. I still skate with these same skates.

Today at the rink where I skate someone will say to me, "Those skates look pretty old."
I smile, look down at my old skates and say, "Yeah, I guess they are."
I guess in this throw away world I must be an oddity,

Skating with me was a passion, one like I've never had before or since. I skated every day, 7 days a week in all kinds of weather. The cold at minus 20 degrees below zero didn't bother me. Most of the time I skated alone or with a couple of friends. I would try to come early so as to be the first one on the rink so that I could skate as fast as I wanted without fear of hitting any of the other skaters. Often we stayed after the rink closed and would help to scrape the ice for the next day. After we finished the clean up we would start to skate again as hard and fast as we could.

The rink was circular and the size of a football field. Music, like the "Skaters Waltz" would float from the speakers and other times something fast like "In the Mood." The music really lifted your spirits. The rink was also a social place and the only place where boys and girls could meet in the winter. I rarely skated with girls, preferring to practice my stride and balance. Skating lasted from 7:00 to 9:00 pm weekdays and from about noon to 9:00 pm on weekends. Between school and skating I was rarely home in the winter. My school assignments suffered. When I got real tired after skating I would skip my homework but I managed to squeeze by at school.

I know that there were other happy moments in my life at the time, but I don't recall them. But I do remember that the days on the rink, like those playing ball were the happiest memories of my life. I was doing what I really wanted and I was good at it. Those moments don't come that often in life. But the joy of skating has stayed with me for over 60 years. When I skate now, I really don't care how many people are on the ice, for in my mind's eye I am back on that rink of yesteryear, I am young, my skates are new and once more I feel that rush of emotion. I was a champion speed skater then, the best in my city. When I stepped onto the ice I could feel a surge of power running through me. It was exhilarating. I was champion for five years and earned five trophies. It should have been six but one year I tried to be cute and instead of staying in first place, I dropped back with the idea of coming on strong in the last lap. However, when I tried to pass the first skater, he made a large swath with his right foot and tripped me. I got up and finished second.

The races were a big event, lasting the entire day and took place during the latter part of January. The races were open to all ages from peewees as up through age 18. We skated in two- year age groups, i.e. age 10-12, 12-14, 14-16 and 16-18.

We skated three races 220 yards, 440 yards and 880 yards. Actually we skated six races because you had to skate in a heat or elimination and if you qualified in the heat you were allowed to skate in the final. On the short races you had to get a really quick, fast start. Sometimes one step off the starting line could make the difference of winning or losing. The longer races were more of an endurance contest.

Newspaper reporters were there keeping score for their papers (there was no television then). Results were published in the papers the next day. I really wasn't interested in the publicity, nor the trophy. In fact, one year I didn't pick up my trophy until March, It was the thought of winning, of being the best. I was a speed skating champion.

I happened to pick up a local paper in 2003 and they have a column there of what happened on that day 25 years ago, 50 years ago and 75 years ago. Lo and behold in the 50 years ago column, there I was winning first place at the local speed skating races.

Looking back over my life I realize that I was always searching for that same rush of power that I had felt in my youth when I stepped out onto the ice the day of the races. That search to relive the feeling of speed and the feeling of being empowered stayed with me throughout my life. As I look back over my life I realize that the desire for speed in every aspect of my life caused me tremendous heartache and much disappointment along the path of my life.

I still like to skate fast. Each year I go to Lake Placid with a friend of mine and we skate the Olympic Oval where Eric

Heiden won 5 gold medals in the 1980 Olympics. Speed skaters can only skate from 4:00 to 6:00pm. Today, I'm sitting in the clubhouse putting on my skates. They are over 60 years old. As I tighten the laces of my skates a rush of anticipation comes over me. I have it each time I put on my skates. As I go onto the ice I stand there for a moment looking at the size of the Oval, the Olympic Oval. It's an awesome and beautiful sight. I can feel the history here, how Eric Heiden set world records against the best skaters in the world, the Dutch, the Germans and the Norwegians just to name a few. I wonder too, if I had trained and competed in the 1952 Olympics, would I have been able to win? Back then at age 16, I was two seconds off the world's record in the short races.

It is cold about 20 degrees. A wind is blowing across my face and the sun is beginning to set. It gets colder and I am lost in this moment going fast and I am sixteen again.

HOW ONE MAN CHANGED MY LIFE

I went to an all boys' school. I am a senior in High school now and my homeroom teacher is named Brother Ephrim. He was short, and wore glasses. His eyes always darted about the room at each of us when he taught. He could tell instinctively if you knew the answer to his questions. He would call on you at just that moment and that made you feel quite good, that you had participated in the discussion. He had taught my father at the same school many years before. Now he was much older and almost ready to retire. During the last period of the day we had a study hall. It was a time to start our homework. Throughout the year, Brother Ephrim would come and sit with each one of us and talk to us about our interests and what we planned to do when we graduated We did not have a guidance counselor. One day he sat with me and said,

"You are very bright. I made an appointment for you to have an interview at the College. You are to report at 1:00 pm. at the Main Office."

There was a small Teachers College in Plattsburgh. It had three programs at the time Teaching, Nursing and Home Economics. The entire College consisted of one large building, Hawkins Hall, and two small temporary 'chicken coops' as we called them. I remember wearing a checkered tan and white jacket which had a large hole in the left sleeve. I was really ashamed to go into the office but I didn't want to let my teacher down, so I mustered all the courage I could find and sat down in the office. A nice woman conducted the interview. I filled out an application, signed it, and she said she would let me know the outcome in a few weeks. I held my right hand over my left sleeve the whole time of the interview so that the woman would not see the hole in my sleeve.

Later that day I met my friend, Tom, and we talked. I told him that I had had the interview at the College. Tom was going to work on the railroad when he graduated. His father worked for the railroad and he was assured of a job when he graduated. I had asked him if he could also get me a job. He said that if I started out on the track gang repairing the rails, slinging a 20-pound sledge hammer all day, then maybe they would hire me on a permanent basis.

Looking back now I see the difference Brother Ephrim had on my life. He was a special man, a man of Spirit whose only mission was to help others on their way through life. I know I was afraid of scheduling an interview at the college. The thought of going to a big institution of higher learning intimidated me. I simply would not have had the courage to do it myself. Brother Ephrim looked into my soul and he knew I was afraid and that I needed that extra push to get started.

He helped thousands of young boys like myself to see their potential and what they were capable of doing with their life. I do know that I would not be at this point in my life, writing this story had not one man, Brother Ephrim, sat down with me that day.

MY WIFE

June 19, 1954. I want you to meet my wife Olivia. She is petite, with brown hair and brown eyes, very intelligent, highly intuitive, with boundless energy. She worked side by side with me and her income helped us to move from Upstate to Long Island to Westchester and back to Long Island. She made it possible for me to attend graduate school at Columbia University and Fordham University. She became a self- taught bookkeeper, then attended the university and received her degree in Accounting. In 1965, she studied Fashion Design at Fashion Institute of Technology. In high school she had taken an aptitude test that said that she would excel in any type of creative endeavor. She graduated from Fashion Institute of Technology in Manhattan, Suma Cum Laude, and then worked for various fashion houses in New York City until 1975. Then, she and her partner opened their own business called Meleny Road Juniors at Broadway and 37th street in Manhattan. She manufactured junior dresses and sold them to Department Stores throughout the country.

A few years later she attended Long Island University where she earned a Master's degree in Art History.

She traveled back to her home in Plattsburgh NY and had planned to spend her years painting and taking art workshops. But fate took a hand. With $100, she and four other women founded the Arts Council in Plattsburgh. Now, ten years later the

Arts Council is a flourishing organization. Under her impetus, the Council bought an old 1923 movie theater. She is in the process of restoring it to its original grandeur.

We are not together now, though we share a bond, unspoken. It's just there, and spans 60 years. We care for each other still. We rescue each other in times of need.

THE MILITARY

I had yet to pay my debt to the Armed Forces so I joined the Army on a short tour of duty, followed by a six- year commitment in the Army Reserves. I joined in Manhattan because I wanted to be in a clerical unit. That was great except that I had to travel to Manhattan every week for Reserve meetings.

I met a great group of guys there. Each of us had a dream. I wanted a Ph.D. degree, Bob Browning wanted to be a lawyer, and Joe Danberry wanted to be successful entrepreneur. It turned out that each one of us realized our dream.

Bob was an amazing fellow. He rarely slept except for a few hours. Nighttime was the only free time we had, so he read in the bathroom. It had the only light in the barracks. One day we went to the library together. He pulled the books he had read off the shelves. I was blown away by how much knowledge he had gained.

Joe, on the other hand was a 'good time' guy. One day he said, "I can stand at the corner of Broadway and 42nd street and within twenty minutes I'll meet someone I know." We took him up on the bet. Sure enough he did meet a friend of his walking down the street. We used to call him 'Mr. Broadway.'

Joe lived in Brooklyn, Bob in Queens and I lived on Long Island. When we got a weekend pass, we would all meet at a bar on 42nd street. We would meet about 7:00 pm on Sunday so we could be back by midnight. One Sunday night Bob and I were at the bar sipping beers until after 8:00 pm. and Joe still hadn't shown up. We started to panic, afraid that we wouldn't be able to get back before midnight. That was a guaranteed Court Martial. So like two crazies we ran onto 42nd street and Broadway-Times Square and started flagging cars down asking them if they were going to Fort Dix.

We did this for about a half hour. Looking back we were lucky that weren't arrested. That night lady luck came by in a beat up old Plymouth. A Hispanic American was driving dressed in an Army uniform. He stopped and we begged and pleaded with him to take us to Fort Dix. He agreed. We got there about five minutes before midnight.

The Sergeant at the desk was already filling out the Court Martial papers and would have served them if we had arrived just five minutes later.

The next day we found out that Joe had an accident on the Brooklyn Bridge and didn't make it back until the next day. It was nothing serious, just a fender bender.

I still remember, but mainly the good times.

Our commanding officer was a real wacko. During inspections we had to place our boots on top of our footlockers with the tips showing over the edge 1 inch. He was such a nut job that he made us shine the soles of our boots so that he could look up and see the nice shiny soles 1 inch over the edge of our lockers. He was such a 'crazy' that he was written up in the one of the biggest New York City papers. The latest we heard was that he was being transferred to Alaska. What he didn't know and we never told him was that one of the men in our outfit was from New York City and had an editor friend on the staff of the paper. So we helped the Captain along his hew career path to Alaska where he could practice his craziness in the nice cold weather. I always wondered how the wax on the soles of the boots of the soldiers would look like in 30 degrees below zero weather, if it looked different, or maybe even freeze and fall off.

I learned to be inconspicuous in the military though I did get into trouble one time. We were on bivouac at Fort Dix in July. By the third day I was covered with sand, sweaty and longing to get clean again. I figured out that the only thing moving in and out of the area was the garbage truck after meal times. There is an unspoken rule that you never volunteer. I decided to break that rule and volunteered to take the garbage cans and put them in the back of the truck, ride back to base and unload them there. After I unloaded the garbage cans I decided to grab a quick shower.

While I was taking my shower and singing, one of the sergeants in the building came in and shouted, "How dare you take a shower. You should be on bivouac." He then told me to get dressed and took me to the grease pit. There is a grease pit in back of each mess hall where all the cooking grease collects in a pit about 2 ½ feet in diameter and about 10 feet deep. There is one small brick that protrudes about 3 inches, about 4 feet down. The sergeant put me in the pit and had me stand on one leg on that small brick. One slippery misstep and I would sink into about 10 feet of grease. He gave me a spoon and a can and told me to start cleaning it out. After about a half hour when the truck was ready to go back to base, he told me the punishment was over and that I could go back to my unit. On the way back I noticed that I stunk of grease and would remain that way for the rest of my days on bivouac. I often wondered how it must feel being in combat for weeks and months on end with no relief, with no means of living a normal life, without the small basics, a clean shower, and eating rations from cans most of the time.

After basic training I was assigned to a clerical school where I learned to type real fast and precise. I was assigned to a clerical unit and the rest of my tour went quite smoothly.

My second tour of duty started six years later. It was during the Berlin Crisis. The Reserves were called to Active Duty. My wife Olivia decided to come with me. We rented our house, packed up a few pots and pans and bedding and drove to Fort Bragg, North Carolina.

My first reminder of segregation was the fact that African Americans and white soldiers in uniform, when traveling, would not be given lodging south of Washington, DC. Our unit was from New York City and fully integrated. It was hard to deal with this stark, outright use of segregation.

The second stark realization of segregation came when we were placed on active duty at Fort Bragg. During this tour, I was assigned to a Military Police unit. I quickly found out that the city of Fayetteville was quasi segregated. African Americans lived to the south in the city and whites to the north. As a consequence, we had to form and assign two separate units to patrol the city. We had an African American unit to patrol the African American section of the city and a white unit patrolling the white section.

I was older now in my late twenties. Most of us were older and married and also brought our wives. That created a huge housing shortage. On one weekend alone 12,000 of us reported for duty, looking for a place to live. The first apartment I found was in a basement that was dark and dreary and damp. It was infested with large Palmetto bugs, which really are like cockroaches. This scared my wife to death so I had to find a new place. I wandered up and down the streets of Downtown Fayetteville asking anyone I could find if there was an apartment available and scoured every newspaper I could find.

Sitting in the middle of town was a large, white two-story building with arches on the first level that opened into a group of small shops and booths where vendors were selling their wares.

I asked a nice little old lady what that building was and she said, "Why that's our Market Place. It's our pride and joy." I later found out that the Market Place was where the slaves were bought and sold during the period of slavery in the South. I realized then that I was in a place that really hadn't changed much since the Civil War, that still believed in the old way of life, the way it was during the pre Civil War years, hoping that somehow it would all come back again. Change is difficult here. It was like the changes that occurred after the Civil War never really happened.

I was lucky and saw an apartment for rent in the local paper. I got up at 5:00 am and found the street and the building where the apartment was located. I stood in line, the first one near the door. By 7:00 am there were at least 20 to 25 persons lined up behind me, and as the day wore on the line got longer. It was like waiting in line to see a Broadway show.

When the landlord opened the door I said, "I'll take it" and wrote a check for the deposit and first months rent. I turned out to be a nice first floor apartment, clean and with plenty of sunshine.

I knew nothing about police work. Being in the Military Police wrecked havoc with my psyche. Now I was carrying a club and a 45-caliber pistol. I really couldn't see myself hitting someone else with a club to subdue them or having to draw my pistol and shooting them, though I knew It would be necessary if faced with a life or death situation. Fortunately, I was assigned clerical duties in my unit and never had to use my club or draw my weapon.

Remember the rule, never volunteer. Well for a second time I violated that rule. Our unit wanted someone to work nights and weekends in the police station in Fayetteville. I thought that this was a great chance to get off the Post so I took the job.

To understand what our duties were like, you had to know what it is like being at Fort Bragg. Fort Bragg is the home of the 82nd Airborne Division. They are the paratroopers or the 'jumpers' as we call them. Most of them are young in their late teens and early twenties. They are motivated to join the unit because they earn extra hazard pay. They had to make one jump each month to keep their special pay status. Each month if you drove up near the open fiends where the jumps took place, you could see hundreds of jumpers making their jumps. Several times I drove there and watched the jumps wondering what it would be like jumping, free fall, out of an airplane, then in split seconds pulling the rip- cord that would open my chute. What if it didn't open? I saw that happen once. It was called a 'candlestick.' I remember getting an awful nausea feeling the pit of my stomach almost to point of vomiting. I wondered what flashed through that soldier's mind when his chute didn't open, that in seconds he would be dead. That thought horrified me and stayed with for years afterward and even today I can see it happening again in my mind's eye.

We were assigned to the local police station in Fayetteville. There were two of us the arresting sergeant and me. My job was to type the forms that could eventually lead to a Court Martial.

The pressure of doing a jump every month creates an emotional need for release. On payday, at the end of the month, the city of downtown Fayetteville was filled with jumpers who were looking for a way to forget what they had to do. There was binge drinking with many of the troublemakers being arrested by the local police, fingerprinted and booked at the precinct and then brought downstairs to us to be booked again by the Military Police. It was really a form of double jeopardy. They usually had to pay a fine and then had to face whatever punishment the military handed out.

I worked with two unforgettable characters, one named Danberger who worked at Rikers Island in New York City and Breaney who was a New York City Policeman and a lightweight boxer. Danberger said that your head got all scrambled up at Rikers and sometimes you had to be as crazy as the inmates. He said that he had to walk the cellblock for eight hours with only a whistle. I could sense the effect this had on his psyche. He was short tempered, often for no reason, unpredictable, and could be quite violent at times. An incident that sticks in my memory was one night when a small Spanish soldier was brought before us. He was just over 5 feet tall and spoke only Spanish. By mistake, he placed his hands on our desk, which was about shoulder high to him.

Danberger told him, "Get your hands off my desk." The soldier responded in Spanish but didn't understand what to do so he left his hands on the desk.

Damberger started loosing it and shouted, "I said get your hands off my desk, now!" Again the soldier did not do as he was told. Suddenly Danberger took out his club, waved it in the air and slammed it on the desk about an inch away from the soldier's fingers. He finally took his hands off the desk and Danberger cooled down a bit, but I could see that the next step would have been to smash his fingers if he didn't obey. What I saw frightened me terribly. At that moment he became like one of the inmates at Rikers.

Breaney was quite different though as unpredictable as Damberger. When he arrested someone he would often challenge him to fight. Since he was a good boxer he would always win. This was a bare knuckles affair, quite bloody at times. One night they brought in a huge soldier, drunk as a skunk and ready to fight anyone and everyone. He must have weighted at least 250 pounds and built like a linebacker.

I quietly whispered too Breaney," I think we are in deep shit this time. What do we do next? This guy will make mince meat out of us."

Breaney stepped down off the desk and approached the man. All the time I was thinking, Breaney, don't try to fight this guy. Without notice Breaney took out his 45- caliber pistol, placed it near the soldier's head, and pulled the trigger. The gun was not loaded. There was just a loud click. The man thought he had been shot and fell to the floor and passed out. Then Breaney handcuffed him and two other soldiers lifted him into the paddy wagon and drove him back to the Post. The years have passed, but these memories remain with me, vivid and real as the day they happened.

This is another funny story. Our MP unit helped patrol the streets of Fayetteville, which is adjacent to Fort Bragg. Often we got an order to clean up the prostitutes in the town. So we went out and arrested a small group and put them in a cell that was bugged. Then all we had to do was to listen to the chatter, which went something like this.

The girls would say, "I wonder why they didn't get Jane or Sue or Brenda at such and such a place?" Someone else would say, "Yeah, and they didn't get Mary Jo or Lula May or Rosie at such and such a place." Then all we had to do was to copy down all the names and places and round up the rest of the group. And I was a soldier.

LIVING IN THE SOUTH IN THE 60'S

It's funny how a memory stays with you. Late one Sunday morning we decided to drive down one of the back roads around Fayetteville. It was a dirt road with cotton balls floating in the soft summer breeze from the cotton fields. As we drove along, we heard music. It was coming from one the cotton fields. A group of African Americans were holding their Sunday service. We stopped and listened for a while to the gospel songs and rhythms and beats of the music. I remembered that during the time of slavery, African Americans could only assemble for worship. It was through music that their burdens were lifted, if only for a short time. That was a special morning that I've never forgotten.

I remember waking into a restaurant where no African Americans were seated. I remember too, there were three bathrooms, one, labeled whites, one colored and one other. The other was for American Indians.

I also learned about the cultural divide that still existed between the North and the South as a consequence of the Civil War. We were housed in the worst barracks on the Post. They were old wooden buildings. It was now October and we had no coal for the stove. Neither could we get any paint to spruce up our barracks. It seems that we were still 'Yankees' living in North Carolina, a state that had seceded from the Union. I guess they felt that we weren't deserving of coal or paint. It gets better and funnier. It seems that there was a Master Sergeant who headed a committee of all the Master Sergeants on the Post. Each month they would hold a meeting and divvy up the merchandise that was shipped in that month. We were not on their list. So we used a bit of Yankee ingenuity. We found out who the Master Sergeant was in charge of the committee. We found out where he lived on Post and what his hours of departure were. Being MP's, we promptly arrested him for speeding. He was a Regular Army Sergeant, a career soldier. The one thing he couldn't do was to get arrested and have charges against him even though they were for minor offenses. So we made a deal, no charges would be filed provided that we got what we needed each month. From then on we lived in harmony with our Southern counterparts.

Those experiences helped me to better understand the racial turmoil spreading across the country. African Americans were claiming their rightful place in society after 100 years of oppression. Simply watching TV wasn't enough.

JACK, BOBBY, MARTIN-THE 60'S

In the late sixties, I taught at Hofstra University on Long Island. There were faculty groups and student groups all protesting the War. Our campus was three blocks from downtown Hempstead. Hempstead had a large African American population. There were protest demonstrations against the War on campus, and there were Black Power protests up and down the street in front of the University. These protests had a special energy. All you had to do was walk the campus and you could feel it. It seemed that the entire campus was electrified. Not only were there war protests but you also had Woodstock in 1969. This added a new dynamic to the campus.

Protestors were openly rebelling against the status quo, the assassination of Martin Luther King, the assassination of Robert Kennedy and the War. The atmosphere was always filled with tension. The Kent State shootings added more chaos. It was as if the whole fabric of society was crumbling.

I still continued to take courses for my Ph.D. and graduated in 1970. I was a college teacher.

WALL STREET

For 23 years I was building a career in Education, step by step, first as a teacher, then administrator then as a college teacher. In 1978 I was ending my marriage and was free to chart my life in a new direction, to find a new passion where I could express and enjoy life more fully. I was a speed skater in my youth and still carried the thrill of going as hard and fast as I could. I was always attracted to Wall Street because of the excitement and rapid pace it offered. I was now age 40, well beyond the age of beginning a new career in a world where young men dominate and older men stay in the background directing and managing these large financial businesses. They climbed their way through the ranks either through hard work or by the hand of someone well placed in the organization that guaranteed a secure future and a good income. I had none of that, yet in my nerviness I decided to give it a try.

I was hired by a large grain company to train as a Commodities Broker. My salary was $100.00 per week, less taxes which was to last for 3 months, after which time I would have enough accounts to sustain my livelihood or be fired. I was in a large room, like a classroom with rows of desks, each with a phone and chair. There were about 28 other men and two women. Almost all of them were in their early twenties. There was one man about my age and we sat next to each other. My phone had WATTS lines which meant that I could call anywhere in the world.

With no one guiding me or telling me what to do I was to make phone calls to get accounts. The phone calls were 'cold calls.' You had to call someone you didn't know and try to influence him/her into opening a trading account. My first day was the worse day of my career life. I froze and couldn't pick up the phone to make a call. Even with all my successes as a speed skater in my youth and my success in teaching and even though I kept telling myself, 'you can do this,' the fear simply got worse.

About 4:00 pm my manager who saw that I was not performing, came over to me and said, "How are things going?"

I lied and said, "Not too bad." My stomach was rolling around like a beach ball in the wind. I instinctively knew that I had one more day, maybe two to prove that I could perform. This was not the Wall Street I imagined. Where was the excitement? Where was the action?

That evening I sat down and sat my imaginary self in the chair across from me and started a conversation.

"You know I've got to pick up that phone and make those 'cold calls.'

My imaginary self said, "Yes I know."

And I said, "What can I do to make this happen? How do I rid myself of this fear?"

My imaginary self said, "I don't have a magic bullet. Just pick up that damn phone and do it." Just then a burst of inspiration came to me. I needed a list of potential customers so that I didn't waste time making useless calls. I rushed out of my apartment to the library and pulled Dun and Bradstreet and Thomas' Register off the shelf and started photocopying the names and phone numbers of the businesses that used the commodity markets, either to trade or hedge their products.

The next day, about 8:00 am, before anyone had arrived, I did pick up the phone and made my first call. Each call became easier and easier. During my first three months probation I must have made 4000 cold calls. I opened a wide range of accounts, a large cocoa and chocolate manufacturer, a coffee roaster, and several farmers who grew corn, soybeans and wheat and used the markets to hedge their products.

A 'hedge' is very simple. Say a farmer spends $2.00 to grow a bushel of corn and say the price of a futures contract for September is $2.50. He simply sells the futures contract at $2.50 and locks in the 50 cents per bushel even though his crop is not fully grown or harvested yet. Then he delivers his corn to the exchange in September. There are always two sides to a transaction, a buyer and a seller. In this case the buyer of the September corn contract takes delivery from the seller and both sides of the transaction are closed.

By the end of my three months probation I had more than enough accounts to sustain and exceed by salary and then worked on straight commission.

I later moved to a different firm. It was 1979 and the gold and silver markets were exploding. The increase in oil prices from $2.30 to $30.00 a barrel had caused high inflation. This oil spike occurred in 1973 and again in 1976. Seizing this opportunity, I called everyone from my lists that produced, used, or distributed gold and silver. Suddenly, like magic, I was salesman of the month. Many of my fellow brokers were wondering how I did it. Then in January 1980, the gold and silver markets collapsed with many of my customers losing money. Some accounts were closed and my income shrank by less than half of what it was the previous year. I learned first hand about the business cycle during the recession of 1980, 81 and 82. I was now struggling just to pay my rent and necessities. It was quite difficult, almost impossible to open new accounts. When money is tight, people do not have extra money with which to speculate. It was only with my hedge accounts that I squeezed by. However, they didn't trade that frequently.

Yet I had a dream of becoming a 'trader,' one who buys and sells using a company's money and is paid according to the profits he generates. The mysterious hand of fate made that dream reality. A hedge fund a few blocks from my office in Tower 2 of the World Trade Center traded US Treasury securities, bonds, notes and treasury bills. They opened an account with me. They wanted a daily briefing on the markets and potential price changes each day. I would go to my office at 7:30 am and photocopy the information on the 'financials' from Reuters News Service and hand carried it across the plaza and up 98 floors to their office (there were no fax machines then).
I did this for about 2 ½ months and one day, Paul, one of the owners and head trader said, "Would you like to come and work for us?" We need someone to hedge our trades."
Without a moments' hesitation I said, "Yes." And I could feel my heart racing like it did when I was speed skating. Here was the action, the excitement I was looking for.
After a few weeks Paul let me trade some of the firms money. I really can't explain fully what trading is like. First there is the extreme leverage. You put down a small amount of capital and control a much larger sum of money. Just to put things in perspective, when I traded a government bond, I used $2000.00 of the firms' money but the contract had a value of

$100,000.00. The price fluctuated on the $100,000.00 not the $2.000.00. There were huge profits to be made and equally huge losses taken if you didn't act quickly and close out a losing position. Sometimes it happened in a matter of seconds. A news item would hit the ticker tape that would contradict an earlier statement, or a report would not meet the expectations of the traders who had factored a certain range in their trading. It could be an unexpectedly large increase or decrease in unemployment. I learned early on not to trade on days when these major reports were issued and thus was able to avoid some really disastrous situations.

So there I was in the thick of things. The adrenalin flowed like a river. At times, my moods alternated from being on Cloud 9 to being in the Depths of Hell. To survive I had to go home and clear my mind of what took place that day, to forget the highs and the lows so that tomorrow I could go back a do it again.

Paul, the head trader, would always come over a pat me on the back when I made a good trade and say, "That was a nice trade." And I felt good.

The next day he was cold and analytical saying, but not saying out loud, 'What are you going to do for me today?'

And that's who I was, a Bond Trader.

ON MEETING LILY

Another twist of fate was about to take place. Here is another day that I will never forget. A few of my broker friends wanted to celebrate Saint Patrick's Day at an Irish pub on Long Island. We decided to meet a Katy Daly's in Massapequa. I was really feeling low and wasn't that interested in going, but I finally arrived late about 8:30pm. There were about 12 of us and we sat at a long rectangular table. Some of the guys were dancing with the girls at other tables, but I sat and sipped a few beers. Seated at the table next to us was a large family who came together every year to celebrate the day. I hadn't paid much attention, just watching the people on the dance floor. I hadn't danced much over the years and lost touch with the latest steps. Disco was now the rage. Anyway at the end of the evening the family next to us started to leave. One woman, a beautiful blonde, came over and said, "Hi." She was getting ready to walk out the door. On impulse I took out one of my business cards, tore it in half and asked her to write her phone number on one half and I wrote mine on the other half. We exchanged phone numbers and she smiled and left with her family. This was March 17th, 1980.

I went back to my commute to Manhattan and was doing well financially. About two weeks went by and I got a call from the woman I had met at Katy Daly's.

I want you to meet Lily. She is attractive with blond hair, green eyes, highly intelligent with a wit that can cut you and 'watch you bleed' as the song goes, a wonderful companion, soft, tender, loving and it was love at first sight. We met for coffee and talked and laughed for about six hours. Funny thing about relationships, time suddenly doesn't exist. Over the next few months we dated regularly, made passionate love regularly and talked and laughed a lot. We were both divorced and this was the 'second time around' for both of us. It's harder to commit to another person now. There is a greater risk that things might not work out. Nevertheless, we both were ready to begin again and set a wedding date for October 20, 1980. We wanted to put some fun in the event so we set the time at 'high noon' like in the movie 'Shootout at the OK Corral.' We decided not to exclude anyone so we invited grandparents as well as babies and all ages in between. The wedding was held at a Community Church and we also decided to hold the reception at Katy Daly's, where we first met. We had the same Irish band that had played that first night. The next day we left for Acapulco and stayed at the Princess Hotel. It is designed like a Mayan Pyramid, a multi- story structure. Peacocks strolled in the lobby with at least four Mexican bands playing on the grounds. There were underground waterfalls, a stage show and long tables of food throughout the grounds. This led directly to the ocean. We spent time sight seeing and saw the high divers from the cliffs. Sometimes they turned out to be as young as 16. It turned out to be a week in paradise. Honeymoons are very special. They are a new beginning, which sets us on a new and untried path.

Lily had three sons from her first marriage. They were ages 14, 12, and 8 so I immediately became a stepparent. The joy of being with Lily was wonderful, but now I had the responsibility of caring for my wife and helping raise three children. The easy carefree days when we were dating suddenly evaporated. Our daily schedules took hold of our lives. Looking back it was one of the best of times. We had rented a house and it became alive, full of energy. Robby, Teddy and John, Lily's sons, always had loads of activities, always moving from one venture to another. The house was filled with rock music each one dreamed of being a famous rock star. Each one had his own stereo and John had an electric guitar. When all of this was going at once it was like being at music concert. I had never paid much attention to rock music but I became expert on the latest artists and their music.

Several times a week Lily and I would go to Jones Beach. We would walk along the boardwalk and do some people watching and catch up on the day's events. Here we had the quiet time to recharge our energies. I still remember the smell of the ocean, the spray that sometimes came up on us when the wind blew. The ocean has an awesome energy powerful and majestic. You feel alive in a special way. The air is pure and invigorating. When you are not walking, your body rhythms slow down to the slapping of the waves and a special calm spreads over you. I can still close my eyes and recapture that feeling. I didn't know it then but for the next 28 years I would be searching for that same calm feeling, not knowing exactly what it was I was looking for. It would take my days in prison to figure it all out. But I'm jumping ahead of myself.

COMING HOME

In 1995, I got a call from my brother saying that he had placed my mother and father in a nursing home because they were unable to care for themselves. We have three nursing homes here and this one is the smallest and is run by the County. My brother had researched each one and felt that this one offered the best care. The Administrator is a young man in his 30's who spends and great deal of time reviewing and choosing only those persons who have a dedication to care giving.

When I walked into the house everything was just as they left it. My mother's unfinished knitting lay on the sofa. My father had an easy chair and a table with a radio with a cassette recorder. He loved music and his tapes were neatly stacked in two piles one was for the tapes he had already recorded and the other was of blank tapes for new recordings. I noticed that he had labeled all of his tapes but one, the one he probably intended to label that day. It was as if they had stepped out for a sandwich and would be back any minute, but I knew they were not coming back, ever. They had taken the last step in life's journey and would die in the nursing home. The thought horrified me and drove a bolt of fear through my body that someday perhaps, no almost certain, that my life would end this way.

My father was unable to walk. His knee joints had disintegrated and the doctors said he was too old for an operation. My mother had several choking attacks and had to be rushed to the Emergency Room every few months. My brother lived and worked in Glens Falls about 100 miles away and would be called unexpectedly because one or the other or both my parents were in the Emergency Room. This went on for at least three years prior to the move to the nursing home. My parents were stubborn and fearful. They refused to sell the house and move downstate with my brother. So they stayed alone and in constant fear of what would happen next. They also had refused to transfer ownership of the house to the children. As a consequence, the house had to be sold and the money was used to pay for their care in the nursing home. They were each allowed to keep up $1700.00 for burial expenses and $3300.00.

The first time I walked into the nursing home to visit my parents it had an odor, not a bad odor, but rather stuffiness, like the air was not circulating properly. That proved to be true because all of the windows were closed for safety reasons. My mother and father were in the same room. When I entered I felt that stuffiness and lack of fresh air. I quietly went to the window and opened it slightly and pulled the curtain over it and I told my mother not to tell the nurses so there would be fresh air while they slept.

I went to the nursing home every day and every day I would sit and listen to my mother and father tell stories, many of which I had heard many times before. I didn't realize it then but in telling their stories they were telling me who they were. The stories we tell, tell who we are.

I'll take my father's stories first because he was more vocal and always monopolized the story telling times. He had a kind, gentle heart though he tried not to show it to us. I guess he thought it was a sign of weakness, but in describing him that is who he was a kind and gentle man. In the spring, summer and fall he would take my brother and I fishing or hunting. We would often walk for miles in search of pheasant or squirrels, which we rarely found. My father really was not a hunter like the other men in town. He never had the instinct to kill anything. So we would always come home empty handed, having left the woods as they were. But his gentleness had shown through and that's how we got to know him. For if you watch what a man does you see who he is.

He told me of his early years when he had to give all of his money to support the family and wasn't given any. This made its mark on his psyche because he never once asked us for money when we were working. Then came the Depression. He was a color mixer of pigments for wallpaper designs. He told me about his need to move from city to city to Buffalo, then Chicago to find work. He told of living in rooming houses and eating at greasy spoons in order to send as much money home as possible. But when it came to mixing colors he was animated to the point that I could see he was doing it again right there in front of me.

He would tell me, "Gray is a very tricky color. It either has red or blue in it and you can never go from one to the other". He would say, "Look at that gray wall, its got blue in it". Then he would tell me about the yellows, that there are two yellows, one a soft or lemon yellow and the other an intense cadmium yellow. And the blues were the same. There are two blues, one a clear sky blue or Persian blue and the other a dirty greenish Prussian blue that can't be exchanged one for the other. And one by one he went on about colors and how tricky it was to figure out how much of a color to add to the mix.

By telling me his story, he was telling me, "You know I'm the best there is when it comes to color mixing." That was who he was a color mixer.

After years of working with the color pigments, the chemicals in them caused my father to develop a severe rash on his hands and he had trouble breathing as well. Eventually he had to quit his job. Believe it or not, his next job was as a machinist at a local factory that made razor blades. He was a self- taught machinist learning one machine at a time until he mastered every one in the shop. He then moved to the local paper mill where there were large rubber coated rollers about one and a half feet in diameter and about 18 to 20 feet long. As the paper was being processed, it would pass between two of these rollers with only a few one thousandths of an inch in between. The machines ran 24 hours a day 7 days a week. The heat and wear would make the rollers uneven. The machine had to be broken down and the rollers ground down. My father would tell he how he shaved only one or two thousandths of an inch from a roller and made it perfectly round again and you could see how proud he was when he told this story. My father was a machinist.

My mother was a special woman though quite different. She was stoic, always there like a rock, and the stronger of the two. She was an accomplished pianist having studied at a Conservatory and would sit for hours playing the popular songs of the day. We would hum or sing along if we knew the words. In her later years she developed Rheumatoid Arthritis and her fingers became all twisted, so finally she had to give up her piano playing. I took piano lessons for several years until I got into a disagreement with my teacher and quit.

My mother had a second passion that lasted until the day she entered the nursing home. She was an avid crafter. She knitted beautiful multicolored Afghans, mittens, scarves, gloves, slippers and potholders just to name a few. She crocheted doilies, center- pieces and borders around napkins and towels. She also made patchwork quilts from scraps of left over fabric. She would give many of these items to as gifts at Christmas Time, thus saving the expense of buying them. My mother was not an especially good cook, though she had two specialties, one was her turkey stuffing that we had at Thanksgiving and the other was her fruit cake that we had at Christmas.

My mother told her stories. She would tell me that as a young girl she was never allowed to sit alone with a boy and was chaperoned wherever she went. She told of the times that she skipped away to go to a local dance until she get caught by her father who was waiting for her and how that finished her 'tripping the life fantastic.' But she would always have a twinkle in her eye and the glee that comes when we are young, like as if she were reliving it again right in front of me. She told of leaving home and going to work in the paper mill where she met my father. They were working across from each other picking paper plates off an assembly line and how they began dating.

Then she said one day out of the blue my father said, "Let's get married" and they did. She never talked about the hardships, the lack of money in the early days, of being separated by my father's travels to find work or of any ailments she may have had. Here stories are different from my father's, fewer but you could tell that she spent her life in the shadows doing her crafts to keep busy. It was by what my mother did that I got to know who she was.

While in her sixties with the household needing extra money, she took a job as a waitress at the local Woolworth store. She loved to tell about her customers and who would order what from the menu and who was a big tipper and who was not. She got the inside scoop on the local gossip. She would tell me about so and so, and what was going on in their lives. But in the telling of these stories she became animated and I could see in my mind's eye my mother serving coffee and breakfast to her customers and chatting about the events of the day. She was telling me and not telling me out loud that she was a good waitress, that she cared about her customers, that she enjoyed the interaction with them. She laughed a lot and was happy doing what she was doing.

And I listened. And that's who my mother was.

They passed away, my father in 1996 at age 86 and my mother in 1997 at age 88. I cried then with deep sadness and realized that I was truly alone, that I could no longer pick up the phone and tell my mother the ups and downs in my life and even now the tears come back as I'm writing this.

MY ENERGY WORK

So far, as you are reading this you are probably wondering; why does this story need to be told? There is a powerful change about to take place.

In 1996, I was invited to attend a convention by my friend, Tom.
I said: "Tom isn't dowsing all about finding water?"
He said: "No, you will find that most of the discussions will be spiritual in nature."
So I decided to go with him. We attended classes from 8:30am to 5:00pm for four days with an hour lunch break. There were evening activities with music. One evening an Indian Shaman led us in drumming, dancing, and a walk through a labyrinth with a bonfire in the center. We placed our intentions in the fire and thanked the Spirits for being with us. The feeling is hard to describe. It was as if we out of our bodies and were floating to the beat of the music.

Those four days changed my life. Something had always been missing. It was like I was looking for a piece of me that was there but somehow got lost over the years of work and worldly desires. I longed for inner peace, just to set my ego aside and be me, who I truly am.

I learned how to use a pendulum and to ask yes or no questions. I learned about Spirit Guides and Angels. During the following years I read hundreds of books on all different topics i.e. reincarnation, Buddha, Taoism, Toltec, Shamanism, Hinduism, the Kabala, karma, just to name a few. I studied the works of Emoto and his work with water crystals. Also, I studied Ernest Holmes and Jose Silva's mind control theories. In the pure sciences I studied the works of Einstein, Jacques De Benveniste and William Tiller all of whom offered scientific proof that the universe has a consciousness and that we can communicate with it. This opened up a whole new vista. It changed the way I thought. I had always believed in God, and came to realize that what I was searching for, the greatest minds in history were searching this same path.

Throughout this time I still had doubts and my ego was still in control. It was my ego that created the doubts that prolonged my transformation.

Ego, "You can get yes and no answers from you pendulum but they are not always right."

Me, "Yes, I know."

Ego, "You must use you will power. Look at all you've accomplished using your will power."

Me, "Yes I know, but I don't think this works the same way."

Ego, "Yes it does, trust me. Have I ever steered you wrong?"

Me, A small voice kept saying, "I still don't think I can do this using my old ways."

I kept reading books and attended the yearly convention of the Mystic Society. 1998 was a road marker in my transformation. While at the Convention, sitting on a bench after dinner one night, I started talking with the man sitting next to me. His name was John Banks and he was from British Columbia. As we talked, he recounted his experiences, casting out negative spirits and helping to clear a person's energies, removing the negative energies and adding positive energies to replace them. He was confident, sure that his dowsing would achieve success. I was fascinated with him. I had always doubted my dowsing and often got wrong answers. John was so unusual that he dowsed the color of cards face down with a score of 50 out of 52 correct answers. I knew then that I had met a truly gifted dowser. John and I kept in contact and shared knowledge.

That year we had a special evening program, so special that it is etched in my memory. We learned how to bend spoons using our intent. Using the focus of the group we were able to bend re-bars that are used in highway construction. We were able to lift a 250- pound man sitting on a chair with our finger- tips. We learned how to break boards using our intent. I went home that year with a new sense of purpose. I wanted to improve the success rate of my dowsing.

Ego, "You did great at the Convention. Just keep at it."
Me, "I don't know. It seems like I don't need my will power, but rather to focus on the outcome as if it's already done."
Ego, "No, you still need your willpower."
Me, "I'm not listening to you. You've helped me but I need to be free of you on this one."

I told my friends what had happened at the Convention and they just smiled.

This segment is difficult to describe because the changes that were taking place were internal and not visible to anyone else. Old ideas were discarded and replaced by new ones. For example, I learned that I was not alone with my ego, that I had Spirit Guides and Angels helping me. My Spirit Guides didn't do the work for me, but through intuition, they slowly moved my thinking into a new direction. My ego resisted all of this and wanted to keep control of my mind. The battle at times was intense. My ego was telling me to use will power to dowse and ask questions and my Spirit Guides were telling me to let go and trust in their guidance. I had used my ego throughout my life to achieve my goals. Trusting in my Spirit Guides was a struggle of monumental proportions. To move from the known and tangible to the unknown and unseen seemed so difficult. Even though my readings and intuition were telling me which way to go, I often reverted back to my old ways, looking for concrete proof for everything I was doing. Trusting and letting go are the keys to spiritual development.

To bridge the gap and to gain concrete proof, I kept bending spoons, using first a teaspoon, then a soup- spoon and then tablespoon. In this way I was able to strengthen my intent and at the same time strengthen my belief that I could control these unseen energies. This gave me a new sense of confidence in my abilities. Subconsciously, I knew that these energies were alive that they had a consciousness and that I could communicate with them through my intent.

I desperately wanted someone to collaborate my ideas and then I remembered a passage from the Bible, "Ask and ye shall receive." So I put out a request to the Universe to meet the right person who would further my development. My request was answered in 2001 at the Convention. There I attended a class by Samuel Grayson. He confirmed everything that I believed in.

In 2005, I attended a conference given by Dr. Masaru Emoto in Montreal, Canada. A discussion of his work can be found on the Internet. He is a foremost Japanese scientist who, after thirteen years, was able to create his technique of working with water crystals. His theory is that words have energies. Beneficial words like love and peace and joy have beneficial energies and words like hate and war and greed have non-beneficial energies. To test his theory, Dr. Emoto taped the word 'love' on a bottle of water. He then froze the water, then thawed it slightly and found to his amazement that a beautiful crystal had formed. He did the same with the words peace and joy and found again that they produced a beautiful crystal. He then tried famous people like Beethoven and Hitler and found that Beethoven created a beautiful crystal while Hitler created no crystal at all and was dark in color. Dr. Emoto's work confirmed two important ideas, one was that words have energy and the other was that water holds the energies of the words.

I decided to take this a step further. I wanted to raise the energies of water. If, with intent I could bend spoons, then it seemed logical that I could raise the energy of water with intent. I would first measure the energy field of the water. Then I would use intent to raise the energy. Then I would measure the energy field again. In every case the energy field increased. This again proved two ideas; one that water has energy and two that we can change the energy of water with our intent. I concluded that water is alive and has its own consciousness.

Then a truly astoundingly amazing thing happened, although when you believe in your Spirit Guides and Angels nothing is so amazing. Back in 1975, I wrote a book with Larry Rashel while teaching at the university.
When I left teaching and went to Wall Street, I lost touch with him and hadn't heard from him for 30 years.

Then on January 21, 2005 an email was in my inbox which read, "Hi, I Googled you. How are you doing? Love, Larry." After 30 years this was no coincidence. There are no coincidences in the Universe. Each significant person you meet is there for a purpose. Larry came back into my life for a reason. I knew that. It didn't take long to figure out what it was. I answered Larry and asked how he was doing. He answered back that he is living in Palm Beach and teaching workshops throughout the world on 'mind clearing.' and sent me a copy of his material. At that point I knew what was happening. I had been reading, developing a framework of my own concepts and ideas but had not put the material together. Suddenly, as if a bomb exploded in my mind, I knew that I was ready to teach my material to a wider audience. That day I sat down and wrote my workshop and finished it within a few hours. The next day, using my skills from my brokerage days, I got on the phone to potential sponsors. Within a few hours had locked in four dates for my workshop. This, to me, is a clear example of how the Universe works. The Universe had given me all the information and skills I needed to make this giant leap and all I had to do was act on it. If I had to summarize the process of working with intuition, it would involve the key elements of belief, intent and action. First you must believe in what you are doing. Second you must use your intent to communicate your ideas to the Universe and finally you must act on your beliefs. Without action, nothing happens.

The next week I created my own website.

I traveled up and down the East Coast doing my workshops in New York City, Long Island, Boston, New Hampshire, Vermont and Montreal, Canada. The highlight of that year was my workshop and presentation to the Mystic Society in Vermont.

With each class I gained new insights, which kept me searching for answers to a myriad of questions that sprang into my mind. It was a spiritual awakening like no other in my life. It was also the time I met Alice Brown. She was, witty, attractive, charming and fun loving. But I'll leave the rest of this story for a later time as it bears directly on my present circumstances.

Looking back, I recognize that much of what I did in 2005 was still ego driven. The restlessness that had been with me for my whole life was still there. Intuitively I knew that something was missing. I knew I hadn't yet given my ego the 'old heave ho.' That was to be the next step in coming to that place where peace and joy ruled my life.

Before that happened, however, I was to experience a new baptism of fire. Now in my 71st year, 2006, started out to be just a routine time. I decided to pull back and do more reading and research and spent less time giving workshops. I still continued to give workshops in Vermont, Montreal, Canada and the Mystic Society. Of all the places I visited, the Montreal workshops proved to be the most rewarding. Susan Trossler is the director. She is a medium and clairvoyant. Students from all over the world come here to study and follow the spiritual path. It is here that I met Jim, a clairvoyant, spiritual teacher. We became friends and decided to collaborate on this book. The stories he tells about are real life experiences from his extensive background. We've used this material to create a contrast between my ego driven life experiences and Jim's that are spiritual and originate from his ability to see into the future.

There is one workshop that I gave at Franklin County, Vermont that has an unusual twist. Ruth Wilson was the President and our host. I was to give a lecture on Friday evening with the workshop to follow on Saturday and Sunday. On Friday, a powerful thunderstorm cut the power lines and we were left in the dark. I had to give my lecture and demonstration by candlelight. It was a failure. In fact, I registered it as a giant disaster. My demonstration of energizing water and raising its energies was not successful. Throughout my talk, I felt as though I was choking and could barely finish the evening's material.

The next day before the workshop began I told Ruth what had happened.

She said, "You know, there is a spirit in this church." We were in a church

She said, "Do you see that picture of a woman? Look at her eyes."

When we did, we saw a fierce, intent stare at us as if she was alive behind the picture.

Ruth said, "I believe that it is her spirit that is here." Ruth, who is a master dowser, communicated with the spirit and asked it to leave and move to its next level of spiritual development. The spirit did not acknowledge Ruth's request. Ruth then asked the spirit to move to the back of the room and into the kitchen. The spirit agreed to do so. She then asked the spirit to leave. At the end of the day the spirit still had not left.

Meanwhile, I was ready to start my workshop, yet I didn't seem to have any energy. Another woman in the group was trembling and was nauseas. I asked Ruth to check our energies. She did so and found that we had no energy field! She then proceeded to draw energies back into our fields and we were able to continue for the rest of the day.

I believed that I was protected from such happenings. To my amazement, I found that the spirit was able to draw away most of my energy field. That left a profound impact on my psyche. I knew then that I needed a new kind of protection, one that guards against this ever happening again.

I called Ruth about two weeks later and asked what finally happened. She said that she returned to the church and that the spirit had left and that the painting had 'mysteriously disappeared.' This whole experience certainly made me a believer in the Spirit world.

I learned a valuable lesson. If a Spirit could drain the energy from my energy field and had such a negative impact on my being, then there must be more powerful Spirits who could provide me with positive energy. I had no doubt now that my life would change forever. It was then that I recalled a line from the Revelation. John said, "God is spirit." I asked for the 'Spirit of God' to enter my mind, body, spirit and energy field. I did the same for the 'Spirit of Jesus' and the Holy Spirit. I no longer had to pray to God, but instead had the energy of God in my being.

Now my mind was exploding with thoughts and a new way of looking at the world my life. Through dowsing, I asked if there was a 'Spirit of Love' and got a yes answer. So then I asked for the 'Spirit of Love' to enter my mind, body, spirit and energy field.

It was then that I expected a miracle but nothing happened.

Again my ego was telling me, "I told you so. You haven't been following my direction. You've got to use your will power like you've always done."

But deep inside I knew that my ego was wrong, that I had to continue on this spiritual path. For the entire year 2006 I continued this struggle with my ego, going back and forth from my old ways to following my new spiritual path. For me this was not easy since my entire life up to this point had been ruled by my ego. The internal struggle involved changing my belief system. This is the hardest step in the entire process. It's one thing to say that you are changing your belief system, but it's quite another thing to actually do it. The use of will power and hard work had always been my driving forces. To let go of them and trust in a Spirit world to help me was a giant leap of faith. This was the miracle I was looking for, but which did not happen. It would take another year and a dramatic turn of events to finally do it, to follow my spiritual path.

I realized that I was entering a new world, a new dimension now. It is different, not linear like the real world. Time and space do not exist. They are just constructs of man's need to control his life. They are constructs of the ego and they work quite well as long as the ego is in charge. At the point when the ego breaks down and the self takes over, we realize the struggle of life for material possessions is futile, that the only way to peace and happiness is through the spiritual path. There are ways to enter the path more easily. The simplest and most direct way is to do nothing. The ego can't stand it when you are doing nothing. The ego wants you to continue chasing and chasing and chasing after some goal, that after reaching it, the ego keeps you chasing and chasing and chasing after a new goal. This does not mean that you lack direction in your life. On the contrary, you develop stronger and stronger resolve to achieve your goals. You focus on activities that nurture the Spirit, such as Love, Peace, Prosperity, Forgiveness, Prayer, Gratitude, Kindness, Mindfulness, Creativity, Beauty, Joy and Life itself. By setting aside a time each day to do nothing, the ego slowly loses control and these wonderful energies begin to take hold in your life. The process is the same for each person. It is only the time needed to achieve these energies that varies from person to person. You can see I was a late bloomer.

Changes are occurring rapidly now. Each day I stop and do nothing. Each day I sense the core of me getting stronger. There is more peace in my Spirit, less restlessness. My beliefs are getting stronger and stronger. I now believe that beneficial changes will occur in my life, that some of the goals that I have been chasing my whole life will be realized easily and without struggle. I have three primary goals now peace, love and prosperity. By peace I mean the inner calm of my Spirit. By love I mean sharing my life with my partner whom I love unconditionally and she loves me unconditionally. By prosperity I mean both a spiritual as well as material prosperity to do the things I choose but that are always for my best and highest good.

During this time I was also doing small experiments using intent to communicate with other forms of consciousness. My first one involved a group of ants on our deck. We had tried ant powder but it didn't work. So I decided to talk to the ants.

I said, "All of you must leave this deck. I don't care where you go but you must leave." A few days later I went on the deck and many of the ants had gone but there was still a small cluster left. Again I said, "All of you must leave this deck. I don't care where you go but you must leave." About a week later I went back on the deck and there were about 7 or 8 ants left. So I decided on a technique that I used when I was teaching. I used to give anyone who misbehaved three warnings and on the third one I took action. So I decided to try it on the ants. So I said, "This time all of you must leave this deck or you will get squashed." Believe it or not, when I went back a few days later there were no more ants and ants have never come back on the deck to this day. So I discovered that I could communicate with the consciousness of ants and they responded to my intent.

My next experiment was a bit more complicated. We normally placed our garbage in plastic bags near the road. Every Monday morning without fail a large group of crows, seagulls and smaller birds would tear the bags open and have a feast. I decided to place a shield of energy around the bags to prevent the birds from getting to them. I was confident I could do this because I was able to get rid of the ants. To my disappointment it didn't work. I became very doubtful and unsure of my use of the energies. I had always raised the energy or water and was able to measure that change. After several months of frustration I decided to let the project go. One day when I was sitting doing nothing it dawned on me what was wrong. I hadn't raised the energy in the shield to a level high enough to keep the birds away. The next week I placed a shield of energy around the bags with the intent to raise it to the energy to the level needed to keep the birds away. As soon as I did this there were no more birds. The birds were still pecking away at other peoples' garbage on the street. What I learned here was that I wasn't specific enough in my intent. The more specific your intent, the better are your chances of success.

Flushed with these two successes I wanted to go a step further and get all the birds off the street just like I had done with the ants. On garbage day I went outside with my pendulum and started spinning it.

I said the same thing to the birds as I had said to the ants. "All birds must leave this street today." I quickly found out that birds are extremely difficult to communicate with. Since they are not grounded like the ants, their frequency was very different. I kept spinning my pendulum for at least fifteen minutes and nothing happened. Again I renewed my focus and intent and said, "All birds must leave this street today." What I noticed was that they were not all flying in their normal east to west path. They started to scatter and fly off in different directions. Again like the ants, there were some stragglers on the light poles and the rooftops across the street. I kept spinning my pendulum and again renewed my focus and intent and said, "All birds must leave this street today."

Slowly one by one they all left. This process took about a half hour.

The next week I had 4 or 5 stragglers on the light poles and rooftops and they left rather quickly. From then on, on garbage day we had no birds on our street.

This one put me on cloud nine. Then I decided to make a bold move. I used the same idea of the shield and decided to place a wall of energy down the entire street. This way I wouldn't need to worry about the stragglers. This taught me a new and valuable lesson. You are limited in what you do only by the limits of your imagination.

This brings me to the winter of 2006/2007. On December 16th, I moved into an apartment. It had two bedrooms, a living room, kitchen and bath, about 1200 square feet. I am living in Plattsburgh, New York, 60 miles south of Montreal Quebec. Here the winters are brutal with fierce, north winds and temperatures that go to minus 20/25 degrees below zero F. Most days there is a strong wind chill factor that is not recorded in the official temps.

First, I turned off all the circuit breakers for my electric heat. Then, I decided to raise the temperature in my apartment to 72 degrees F. For two weeks nothing worked and the weather kept getting colder by the day. I wore a jacket and insulated pants to keep warm. Then came a point when I decided that either I could do this or I would cease my energy work altogether. About the end of December I suddenly had heat at 53 degree F and noticed that it kept fairly steady at this level. I bought a thermometer to record the temps and at the same time copied the temps for Plattsburgh from the MSN website. Each day I took the temps at 2:00 pm. I further noted the temperature held steady between 53F and 56F except for two blizzards, one on Valentines Day and one on St. Patrick's Day when they dropped to 51F. On both of those days we had fierce north winds that drove the wind chill factor to minus 25 below zero F.

Then I evaluated my results. From February 5 to March 9, 2007, the official temps from the MSN website ranged from minus 21 degrees below zero F to 34 degrees above zero F. These numbers did not include the wind chill factor.

Using my pendulum, I asked my Spirit helpers why I didn't get my 72F. They said they did the best they could do. As usual, I thanked them profusely for all their help.

ALICE BROWN

I want you to meet Alice Brown. Alice is quite attractive with brown hair and big brown eyes. She is charming, socially graceful, and full of fun and laughter. She had the misfortune of having a serious automobile accident. In spite of this she still remained an upbeat person. Her mind is quick and sharp, always with a snappy retort. She could cut you deep with her tongue but her gracefulness mutes her response. She always chooses her words carefully so as not to offend anyone. Her disability caused her to quit her job and retire. Through all of this she still remains optimistic about her life and her future. We met and started a conversation. Over the course of several months we got to know each other. She had been married and divorced and we became good friends. We lived in the same apartment building.

MY TRIAL

What was about to happen next is, to this day, beyond my comprehension. Nevertheless, it did happen and cannot be erased or changed in any way. My emotions were ripped to shreds and my self-confidence shattered in a pile of ashes. I was numb and confused, angry and betrayed, and lost my equilibrium completely. My ever-present ego was nowhere to be found. Yet, now I understand why it had to be this way. It opened the final doorway to my spiritual development. It was disaster turned into peace and love. I'll explain this part later as the story develops.

This is the day that will be etched in my memory forever. In the early morning, about 8:30 am, I was sitting on the steps outside my apartment. When Alice came out I asked her if she would give me five minutes of her time. She walked right past me. I walked over tapped on the car window and asked her again if she would please give me five minutes of her time. She then drove off. Within less than a half hour a State Police car drove up and asked my name.

When I told them, they promptly handcuffed me and said, "You are under arrest for harassment." They drove me to the nearest Police Headquarters where I was booked and fingerprinted.

Then I was escorted by Police car to the Local Court, asked to stand before a Judge who charged me with harassment, a misdemeanor. It was a criminal charge nonetheless. I was so stunned that I could hardly speak. The Judge set my bail and said that I had one phone call. I called my attorney who had recently drawn up my will but he said that he did not handle criminal cases. The Judge then assigned me a Court Appointed lawyer and set the date for my trial that was to be two weeks hence.

So now, I'm here sitting in solitary confinement. I knew that I had to post bail but didn't have anyone with whom I wanted to share my problem, being too ashamed of what happened. I finally decided to call my ex-wife, Olivia. Even though I had heaped a pile of hurt upon her, we had a special bond between us. If either of us were in trouble, we would help the other one out. That she did. She posted bail and drove me back to my apartment. Then she helped me to find a good defense attorney who would take my case. When I called him, he was out of town on a vacation. He didn't return until a week later. When I finally spoke to him, he said that he wasn't doing criminal work any longer but recommended Tom Briscoll. I set up an appointment with Mr. Briscoll just before my Court date. We appeared in Court as scheduled. Mr. Briscoll requested a postponement to give him time to obtain my records from my Court Appointed lawyer to study the case. The Judge granted his request.

During the last week of July and first week of August I was scheduled to give my workshop and speech to the Mystic Society. Over the past year I had done new research and readings and had a new theory of how Mind, Body and Spirit are integrated. I wrote this new material in outline form, which I used in both the workshop and speech.

Though I was under a great strain from my Court case, I rather enjoyed the travel and interaction with the people whom I met at the Convention. It's a time to reconnect with old friends, to tell stories and fill in the events of the past year in each of our lives. It's also a time to say Hi to someone new, to learn about their lives and their passions, to exchange emails and share new ideas. The best part of it all is that we laugh a lot.

Returning home, the days were filled with raging emotions. Why had Alice done this? There was anger, confusion, bitterness, and betrayal, to name a few. Why does Alice want to brand me a criminal? Why did she want to do this at this stage in my life? Was anything I did to her so terrible that it merited this action? The only motive I could come up with was that she wanted money and while in a criminal action she could not sue for money damages, a criminal conviction no matter how small would allow her to file for money damages later in a Civil Action. The strange and bizarre part of all this was that if she needed money all she had to do was ask and I would have given it to her.

I then moved and rented a small, one bedroom apartment in the City. When I left I took only my clothes and my computer as the apartment I was in was fully furnished. I bought some used furniture, bed and chairs and some items were given to me by friends that included towels, washcloths, kitchen utensils, table, chair for my computer, TV and even a small electric organ. The apartment is clean and furnished with new kitchen cabinets, new bathroom, carpeted with plenty of windows, and where I get the morning sun coming in the kitchen. The only one disadvantage is that it is on a busy street and there is some noise from the traffic during rush hours. I am used to it now and its own special rhythm. There is adequate parking and a free washer/dryer, which saved me the expense of having to buy them or having to go a launder mat.

This was the best medicine because now. I was able to sort out my emotions, knowing intuitively that I had to let go of the anger and bitterness that so consumed me in the first week after my arrest. I went back to my old routine of the gym and pool for physical exercise, reading and meditation. It was in those quiet times that I could feel the negative emotions dissipating and my old optimism coming back into my mind, body and spirit. I created a new image in my mind that either Alice would drop the charges against me or that I would be found not guilty. In the event of a trial, I had learned in my energy work that energy follows thought. That explains how your thoughts guide you toward a desired goal.

The next month passed and then the next. My attorney told me that the District Attorney would make an offer of settlement before going to trial. That she did. It was harsh. I had to plead guilty and undergo counseling. At first I believed because I had moved away that Alice would drop the charges and let our relationship die a natural death. That did not happen. I told my attorney that I could not accept the offer and if need be I would go to trial to clear my name.

The next step was jury selection. This was scheduled for the second week of December. If it hadn't been that I was the person for whom members of jury were being chosen, I would have found the inner workings of the justice system quite interesting. 25 to 30 prospective jurors are asked to serve. They were called in before the Judge in groups of eight, six were to be jurors and two were to be alternates.

I want you to meet Judge Black, a woman in her late 50's or early 60's, reserved, with blonde/gray hair, with a soft voice yet direct, with her words carefully chosen. You could sense that she wanted to dot her I s and cross every T, so there could be no challenge to her rulings. First off she read an eleven page set of guidelines to the panel, explaining their responsibilities and the parameters of the case, what evidence they could or could not consider and that as best as possible, rule on the merits of the case and not let their emotions color their decision.

Next, I want you to meet the Assistant District Attorney, Janice Green. She is tall, slender, very young, very attractive, highly aggressive, with a strong need to win, dressed immaculately in a tailored suit, dark maroon, with moderately high heels. She is what one might say nearly perfect. Her voice is well modulated but cutting and sharp. Sitting listening to her, the only thing I could think of is, 'wow, this is one woman I do not want to tangle with.' She asked a set of questions of each potential juror, such as, were they ever involved in a harassment case or did they know of anyone who was involved and what their feelings were about the matter.

Then my attorney Tom Briscoll took over. Tom also is tall, in his late 40's or early 50's, a touch overweight, dressed in dark suit and tie, nothing that would intimidate the jurors. His voice is soft and folksy. He apologized for the late evening hour and thanked each person individually for volunteering to be on this jury panel. He too asked if anyone had knowledge of harassment and how he/she felt about it. He also asked the occupation of each member. One member was a law enforcement officer.
When asked how he felt about the case he said, "He, meaning me, must have done something wrong in order to be here."

Then he asked a question that put some members of the panel in a quandary. He asked, "What if I don't put Robert on the stand. "Would that affect your decision?"

Some members said "No" and some said they wanted to hear my side of the story.

This whole process lasted about an hour. The Judge dismissed the panel to an adjacent waiting room. The Assistant District Attorney, my Attorney, the Judge and I retired to the Judge's chambers. Both the Assistant District Attorney and my Attorney went over each juror's response and whether it merited being dismissed for cause. In other words, was their previous knowledge such that it would color their judgment in this case? It was agreed by both sides that the three persons who had prior knowledge of harassment were to be dismissed for cause. My Attorney then argued that the police officer should also be dismissed for cause because he had prejudged my actions. The Assistant District Attorney was reluctant to do this because she knew that she had one vote for conviction but finally agreed to dismiss this juror. This left four of the eight original members who were then discussed in order, i.e. No 1 juror, No 2 juror etc. So now there were four jurors chosen. We then returned to the Courtroom where eight more prospective jurors were called in. The same procedure of questioning each prospective juror by the Assistant District Attorney and my Attorney was done. Then we again adjourned to the Judge's chambers to review each person in turn. Two more persons were mutually agreed upon to serve as jurors No. 5 and No. 6 and two alternates were chosen as well. We then returned to the Courtroom where all 16 persons were brought in and the Judge named the six jurors and two alternates and dismissed and thanked those who were not chosen. The jurors now were evenly split, three women and three men. Then suddenly one juror raised her hand and asked to meet with the Judge privately in her chambers. The Judge granted her request and the Assistant District Attorney, my Attorney, the Judge, the juror and I, met together. In chambers, the woman said that she had not answered truthfully, that her son had been arrested and convicted of harassment.

My Attorney asked how she felt about this and She said, "It was wrong what he did and he got his just punishment." The woman was excused and now the Assistant District Attorney sensing that she had a lock on her vote for conviction argued vigorously to keep her on the panel. My Attorney argued that she should be dismissed for cause. The Assistant District Attorney then argued that the trial had not started and that being the case, there was no legal basis to dismiss her. My Attorney then requested to read the law book. He did not find the exact sub section that covered these circumstances. Then the Judge asked to read the law book. She found the statute, which did indeed state that the juror must be dismissed for cause and ruled accordingly. This created still another dilemma. Since each juror had a number, the numbering of each juror had to be redone and one of the alternates was chosen as juror No. 6. Then a second alternate had to be chosen from the pool of already dismissed jurors. Both parties agreed to this person.

We then returned to the Courtroom where the Judge announced that one juror was dismissed and named the second alternate. Then finally nearing 10:00 p.m., the Judge dismissed and thanked everyone for spending the time to be here and apologized for the late hour. It was here behind closed doors that my Attorney played a key role in securing, for the most part, a balanced and unbiased jury panel. I can see how, with a Court Appointed Attorneys, who all work for the Court System, that clients would not be as fortunate.

The days and weeks that followed are difficult to describe. On the one hand I still believed that Alice would drop the charges. I had helped her financially and emotionally and naively thought that this would count somehow, that maybe her conscience would tell her this is enough. This did not happen and I had to realize that I had to go to trial, to face six people and be judged by them and that in the end it would come down to a simple yes or no, guilty or not guilty.

I said earlier that Jim and I were not the main characters in this book. Now you will find out who they are. This is magic, pure magic, a magic that Jim knew all along. It was at this point that I did two things that changed my life forever. I stopped writing notes to my Attorney and I let go of all my feelings of bitterness and anger toward Alice.

I said to my Angels and Spirit Guides, 'I'm turning my life over to you now. Protect me and guide me. Take charge of my life. I know you will do whatever is for my best and highest good.'

I had always let my ego take charge. This was the day that unseen entities, my Angels and Spirit Guides became the central players in this drama. I knew then that this had to happen just this way for me to finally let go of the worldly hold that my ego had created. All that I had done or accomplished was an illusion, and that for my whole life I had not listened to them. That is why my whole life was such a mess and why I had to go to trial, why I had to be tested in this way, why I needed such a gigantic kick in the ass to make me listen and live my life in a different way, no longer letting my ego be in control, no longer seeking. I had found what I was looking for, a profound peace and serenity. I had found how to live my life with the most powerful entities, God, Jesus, the Holy Spirit, my Angels and Spirit Guides. From that day forward, my life has never been the same. Everything now is easy. Everything now comes in its own time. This is not to say that I still do not have dreams or goals, but I know that whatever I achieve now is for my best and highest good. If something does not happen the way I planned, that too is for my best and highest good. I see the world with a broader vision and my place in it is where I should be, not where my ego wants me to be. Jim was telling me this all along. He already knew the beauty and serenity that could be found. He knew how to let his Angels and Spirit Guides manage his affairs. I, on the other hand, saw only my ego, only my blind determination to make everything work the way I wanted it to because I wanted to create my own destiny. Yes, I did accomplish a great deal in the material world, yet it was only an illusion, temporary at best, not everlasting the way my ego made it seem. In fact it was all gone now and I was alone living in a small apartment waiting for my trial to unfold. Yet in the midst of this chaos, I now had a new state of existence. I now had something powerful, a creative force that was always inside me but that I never listened to, a force of peace, dynamic and full of life.

I discussed all of this with Jim who just smiled and said, "Yes I know."

The days were running down quickly to my trial date, yet I had a new calm, a peace that let me sleep regularly, a peace that that told me, be not afraid for I am with you. In past situations like this my anxiety would have been almost uncontrollable and fear would have gripped my psyche. That was all gone now and I knew it would never return for the rest of my life.

I had crossed a threshold into the world of the Spirit where love and peace gather, where beauty reins, where joy lifts your spirit and you see each new day as a new beginning, filled with hope and opportunity. The sun shines brighter now. The rain is softer. People seem less rude and angry. It's easy to sit and do nothing now, to let my spirit flow freely in my soul, to give thanks for the many blessings that I receive each day, for life itself. There is a magic to life now, a magic that I never knew existed, a magic of hope, that each new day is better than the one before not worse, a magic that comes from my Spirit not my ego. The ego is capable of all kinds of tricks to keep you believing in the illusions it makes you create. It is a game of smoke and mirrors, that life is simply going from one thing to another to another then to another looking for happiness, which doesn't exist in the material world. If materialism were the answer everyone would be happy. They are not. History has shown this time over time.

As the words to the song, 'And the days dwindle down to a precious few' were ringing in my head, I had to come to grips with the reality of my trial. The words, and my trial were now in my mind. I had seen many TV shows about trials and what they were like and I had read books which depicted the procedures that are followed, i.e. opening statements, direct testimony followed by cross examination, summary statements followed by a verdict from the jury. Our trial system is a binary system. There are only two choices-guilty or not guilty, except of course in the case of a hung jury where jurors cannot agree on a verdict. A verdict of guilty meant that I was branded a criminal for the rest of my life even though it was a misdemeanor. My trial was not at all what was on TV or in books. It was highly personal, about a love affair, about having to tell everyone present and the media, if they decided to print the story, personal details concerning the relationship between Alice and me. Nothing that you read or see on TV can really prepare you for this experience.

Now, the trial date had been set. A small voice in my head still believed that Alice would, at the last minute, drop the charges and that we would still remain close friends. After all, before this happened, though we were not lovers, we were still friends. We were able to chat about the latest stories in the newspaper and on TV, what was happening in our lives. No such luck. The trial proceeded on schedule.

Let me describe the Courtroom. The room had a tile floor, fluorescent lighting which somehow takes away the rosy glow from peoples' faces, two rows of metal chairs with an aisle up the middle and two wooden tables in the first row where Assistant District Attorney, Janice Green, sat on the left and Tom Briscoll and I sat on the right facing Judge Black who was seated high above us, dressed in her black robe.

The Assistant District Attorney wore the same maroon tailored suit she had worn during jury selection. My attorney, Tom Briscoll, wore a dark suit and a non- descript tie. I wore tan slacks and a dark blue turtle—neck sweater. The jury box was on the left of the Judge's chair facing the audience. The jurors were seated up front in the room and to the right of the jury box. I had met with Tom earlier in the morning and he instructed me on what to do and not do. He told me to look directly at the jurors, not to make gestures of any kind while Alice was testifying, not to write too many notes as that would give the jurors the impression that I might be hiding something from them and to answer only with a Yes or No when under cross examination, not to offer lengthy explanations of my answers.

He said that he would lead me to give detailed explanations in his questioning of me prior to cross -examination. I told him that I when I am on the defensive that I freeze up and do not come across well, especially under cross- examination. He said that he would lead me through the key events of my relationship with Alice and that I should be as relaxed as possible.

Assistant District Attorney, Janice Green, called her first witness who was a State Police Officer. His testimony referred to an incident that occurred way back a year ago. My computer had crashed and I had lost all the data on my hard drive. I knocked on Alice's door, wanting to use the disk that I had left with her. When she opened the door she was angry and wanted the extra key to her apartment that I had. I gave her the key and left. I went to our local bookstore to read and relax. When I returned home about 7:00 pm., I got a call from the Police Officer. Apparently Alice had called the State Police barracks and wanted the Officer to give me a warning. I explained to him what happened, that I had given Alice back her key and agreed not to bother her again. On the witness stand, the Officer's testimony was completely different. He testified that, when Alice called him, that he came directly to my apartment, knocked on my door and when I answered he read me the riot. I wrote a note to Tom saying that this was not true, that he never came to my apartment and that I simply received a phone call from him.

On cross examination Tom, in his usual folksy way said, "Officer, were you mistaken about physically going to Mr. Water's apartment, that instead you called him by phone?"

The Officer hesitated then he said, "Now that you mention it, I probably just called Mr. Waters on the phone.

"That's all Officer. I'm finished with the witness," Tom said.

At which point the Judge said, "You may step down."

Next, Assistant District Attorney, Janice Green, called her second witness. She was a Hispanic woman who lived in the apartment building directly across from my building. She testified that I had gone into her apartment building and stood in the hallway near her door for no reason. We were both surprised at this testimony and Tom decided not to cross- examine her.

The third witness was Alice Brown. Her testimony was flawless. Her tone and inflections were like a soft melody. She testified how we first met and that our relationship grew slowly at first and how I helped her, physically and emotionally. But then she said that I was being hostile to her. She said that my asking for a few minutes caused her anxiety and she called the State Police to have me arrested.

Now we go to Alice's cross- examination. I had given Tom at least a dozen instances of interactions between Alice and me that occurred during the prior two weeks before my arrest that showed I had no animosity or any hostility toward her. Tom stood up and started his cross- examination. He seemed rather baffled as to how to proceed. He asked about her background. Then he asked her about her spending the day with me just two weeks before my arrest. Alice vaguely acknowledged this but said that because of her condition she could not remember when it occurred. Tom's cross- examination was very short, only a few minutes. The Judge then called for a ten- minute recess before I was to take the stand. Tom and I went to a small room away from the jury room and down the hall.

We sat down and he said, "We are done for. All we need to do now is to decide on your sentence."

I asked him why he hadn't used all the information I had given him.

He said, "She was so good that I didn't think there was anything to gain by keeping her on the stand any longer."

Now back in the jury room it was my turn. Under direct testimony, Tom led me through the details of my relationship with Alice, how we met, how I helped her. He asked me to describe in detail the day I spent with her a few weeks before my arrest, that we had fun and enjoyed each other's company. That ended my direct testimony.

It was now time for the Assistant District Attorney, Janice Green's cross-examination. She started by asking about the day when I knocked at Alice's door wanting to use my disk for my computer.

She asked me about it.

I said, "I gave my key to Alice and left."

Then she asked the same question again.

I said, " I gave my key to Alice and left."

She then asked the same question a third time at which point I looked up to the Judge.

I said, "I've already answered this question."

She then asked me about entering the apartment across the way and standing in the hallway near the door of the Hispanic woman.

I said, "I really don't know this woman and had no need to go into her building."

Then she asked about the incident that occurred outside my apartment building.

I said, "I was hoping I could catch Alice and have a talk with her. When she came out of her apartment I was sitting on the steps. I asked her if she would give me five minutes of her time. She walked right past me. I asked her again if she would please give me five minutes of her time. She then drove off."

Then Janice Green asked me two questions that didn't seem relevant to the charge of harassment. First she asked me how my relationship with Alice ended.

I answered, "It never ended."

Then she asked how the romantic aspect of our relationship ended

I said, "I gave you love and you threw it away" and I left.

Then Janice Green asked, "Did Alice cook for you?"

I said, "Yes, she did and we had many meals together."

That ended my cross-examination. Then the Judge dismissed me and instructed the jury to start deliberations. The jury left the room and the Assistant District Attorney, Janice Green, the Judge, Tom and I all waited in the Courtroom. I can't describe the thoughts that ran through my mind during the next ten minutes or so. Tom had said that we would lose and it was only a matter of the sentence I would receive. Then I remembered the promise I had made which was to turn over my fate to my Angels and Spirit Guides and whatever the outcome, it was to be for my highest good. That brought back the feelings of peace and calm that I had before entering the Courtroom.

The jury deliberated about ten minutes then came back into the Courtroom. Then, something unusual occurred. They asked for an instant replay of what occurred on the day I was arrested. There was a snafu with the recording and a technician had to be called in to adjust the sound and quality of the tape.

When this happened, Tom whispered to me, "This is not good."

Then the jury left the Courtroom for further deliberations. They returned a few minutes later and were seated.

The Judge asked, "Have you reached a verdict?"

The foreperson said, "Yes we have your honor."

A few days later I went to Tom's office to pay the remainder of my fees. I thanked him for his help and still remember his words. You are done for. What he didn't know was that I sent the energies of love to every person involved in my trial.

Jim and I had a long talk about the way things turned out.

He told me, "Now you see why these tests are put upon you. In your case it was the only way you would surrender your ego and let your Angels and Spirit Guides change your life forever. You are a different person now. You live in Spirit. You will find that your life will never be the same. You are now free to move with the ebb and flow of the Universe. You are truly a free man now. Enjoy it. Live in Peace and Joy."

Jim's Stories

MY FATHER

I started school at 6 years old. It was in the summer time about August when I started to see. On that particular day my brother and I were walking upstairs. My Dad appeared before us in spirit. My brother couldn't see him but I could and I was telling him that my Dad is welcoming me, smiling at me and he's happy and he's moving on. My brother couldn't understand and I remember he said I was crazy. About 15 minutes afterward the phone rang with the news that he passed away. When they were burying him each person threw a handful of dirt over the coffin. When I threw in the earth it was like I could see his face. I didn't say anything but I remember that incident very clearly. Even now, I can remember that incident.

I moved on and went to school. Often Spirit would come to me and tell me certain things or tease me as a matter of fact. While growing up, I was playing and saw this camera. It wasn't the actual camera but I saw the camera in Spirit and after a few days a camera appeared. It did take my picture in the same position that I saw myself before walking across the yard.

After finishing high school I went to college and then I found a job. There were instances of Spirit appearing and they would come when I am praying or during my daily tasks.

THE SEARCH PARTY

When I was in my teens, my ability to see the future came back. I see Spirit and things before they actually happen. In one incident I was with my brother in law. He is a scoutmaster. His name is Herman. He left by boat with a group of boy scouts. Actually we have a sea scullion where I am from. They left for the port that is 100 miles away. He left very early in the morning.

On that particular day I came home early and my sister said to me, "Why are you home so early?"

"No place to go, no girls to see." And I said, "I can't find anybody."

So I puttered around the house and about 8:00 pm I says, "Has Herman arrived yet?"

She says, "No."

When 10:00 pm came I looked at her and said, "Well its time to do something." So I took the boat that we have and I went to my friend and his wife got upset.

She says, "Where are you taking my husband so late at night?"

I says, "Well Herman left with 12 scouts early in the morning and did not return." So we went to go and look for him. We gassed up the boat and got some food and off we went, taking the same path that he normally would take. After 3 hours we had several boats searching but they did not see anything or that any boat was in distress. It was around midnight and the moon was rising. Then about 1:00 am the tide was falling.

So I said to my friend, "Richie, stop the engine and just let me be quiet. Don't say anything to me and let me concentrate. This was my first time trying to meditate in a boat out at sea and somehow I got myself into meditation.

Within ten minutes or so I got out of meditation and said to him, "Go in a West direction."

He said to me, "The tide is falling and that's going to South America."

I said, "Yes we are going towards South America." After a few seconds I said, "Do you see the light?"

He says, "No, I don't see any light."
I said, I see a light and the light is guiding me."

After half an hour we arrived on them and everybody was praying and I told Richie, "I did see the light."

My brother in law, Herman says, "Yes, the battery died and there was a little flicker of light. But that was a good distance away.

So to make a happy ending to the story everybody was cheerful. They ate all the food and we took them home. And that was another story of my life.

RIDING THROUGH THE COCOANUT FARM

Tom and I used to go to the sea, a distance of about 75 miles. On this night in particular we were riding through the cocoanut farm.

I says, "You know Joe, I see a branch coming down and a bunch of cocoanuts coming down hitting the car and as I said so

He said, "Shit it's falling." And I gunned the car, 'petal 'to the metal' as the saying goes. Only one cocoanut struck on the back bumper of the car.

He says, "Shit you saw that before."

I said, "Yes."

He said, "You're freaking my ass out."

And that was another incident.

While traveling that road a whole herd of bison got away from the farm. We had one water bottle and they blocked the road. I wanted to go through and Tom was with me.

He said, "We can't get through that herd. They will kill us."

So I said, "Have faith Tom and we will go."

So I started the car and gently nudged my way through the herd of the buffalo and the bison.

The farm people came out and said, "Did you get through?"

And I said, "Yes."

They said, "Well you took a big chance."

I said, "No, its all right."

They understood and laughed at me.

SPIRIT TAKES OVER

Another time crossing that highway I said to myself, 'Do you know that truck driver is asleep and still keeps the road?' Maybe they are hypnotized or maybe the Spirit enters the body and takes over because Spirit can guide you. If you are asleep and you go off the road Spirit guides you and you will wake up on the other side many miles afterward and you don't know what happened in between. That is what happened to me. I had to cross the road bridges. On one night after I crossed those two narrow bridges I arrived in the village and caught myself.

I stopped the car and washed my face and said to myself, 'I was alone there and how in the hell did I get across?' This was another of my spiritual encounters.

MY FISHING TRIPS

My brother and I bought two boats, one commercial to carry around stuff and one sea type cruiser.

I said, "I will take you and I'll show you the way around the outer islands." I did so and I told my brother a certain thing.

I said, "When its low tide you see certain things and when the tide is high you don't see them."

So that evening my brother says, "Come with us we'll go for a moonlight cruise and we'll go fishing."

I said, "I can't go because I have things to do." So my brother went his way and I went my way. In the middle of the trip about three o'clock in the morning I see my brother over me in spirit.

I said, "What are you doing here?"

He said, "Well I am struck on a rock."

And I said to him, "I told you so" And that is one of the many incidents with my brother with the boat.

We used to go fishing and when we finished fishing everybody would jump into the boat and leave me to steer home to the marker. A couple of times I went through a busy passageway, and you had to stay awake. I found myself heading home instead of the fish market, catching myself turning the helm to go to the fish market and everybody was sound asleep. Again I thank my Spirit Guides for guiding me through that.

SATURDAY NIGHT DANCE

Living close to the sea we lived in the valley. In the hills every Friday and Saturday night you could hear the drums going, and there would be spiritual people singing.

One night I said I would venture up.
The neighbor who knew me said, "Jim is that you?"
I said, "Yes Mrs. Harvy."
She says, "The same way you go up is the same way you come down and whatever you see do not laugh."
I said, "OK Mrs. Harvy."
When I arrived at the place the drummers were going and everybody was dancing and in a trance. I see this very little lady. Actually she was old. She was dancing and got into a trance and she lifted a table with her head. Normally that would take two people to lift it. I was amazed. I was seeing Spirit too and getting into a trance so I stopped and I came back down.
And I says, 'Wow, what and experience!' That was my first experience in a group of people seeing Spirit.

MY OPERATION

I was a sales rep and I was into merchandising. I fell down the stairs in a company supermarket, so I went to my boss and I told him about it.

He said, "Well what happened to you?"

Well I said, " I think I have a hernia."

So he says, "Well go to the doctor and go to the hospital and have it repaired."

My Mom gave me the name of a Japanese doctor. On the day of my appointment he was not there so I had to deal with a woman doctor for the first time in my life. I had never seen a woman doctor. I was amazed and I laughed.

Now, the day came for me to go to the hospital. The head nurse at the hospital was a friend of my sister and I walked in and I told her what I was there for. She told me to go down the hallway and into the room that is facing that is your room. I walked in and I walked back out.

She said, "Is anything wrong?"

And I said as I looked at her, "How long has he been dead?"

And she says, "What are you talking about?"

I said, "The person who was in the room died there."

She says, "There's nobody there and that room is clean."

I said, "Just check your files. The person who was there is gone."

She says, "Are you afraid?"

I said, "No I am not afraid. I said, "No problem, I'll go back in to sleep there." But I also told her, " When I was growing up as a kid we were close of a leper asylum and the leper asylum had been closed. It was a 16 or 17 bedroom mansion. A monk died there. He got killed in a room on the south side of the building. When they would paint the walls, the blood would show up after a period of time. No one wanted to sleep in there because sometimes they would see the presence of the monk and sometimes he would slap them. They dared me one time to go and sleep there. I took up the challenge and I went to sleep in that room. I slept in that room for almost two years and nobody ever disturbed me. It was the simple way that I slept in the room. The natives usually sleep that way. I did not sleep in the bed. I slept in a hammock and the hammock was across the room not to the length of the room. He was happy to have me there." And that's one of my stories of my life of sleeping with Spirit.

HAPPY TIMES/SAD TIMES

Eventually I got married left home and came to Canada.

On my way here an old Indian man met me on the street. He stopped and he says, "Saab, if you give me 5 cents I'll read your hand, the palm of your hand."

So I said to myself 'right' in my mind so I opened the palm of my hand and he read it.

He said, "In a few months I'll be headed to a different land, and that I have a long life span and he says I'll eventually marry and move to that land.

I said, "OK." I gave him the 5 cents and he went on his way.

A few months later I had a dream, but when I dream it's like reality. I will get up in the middle of my dream and I will still be seeing these things. I saw myself talking to an elderly man and we were outside an apartment complex.

I was saying to him, "What a wonderful place. The sun is still out at 9:00 o'clock in the evening. I have never seen that before."

Five years after I arrived in Canada I ended up talking to this gentleman, whom I remembered vividly, and everything that took place. Then after a few months he passed away. I was very sad about that.

Now I was married and I had three beautiful kids. Time came for things to happen.

A year before my wife divorced me I told her, "I know you are going to divorce me."

She looked at me and she said, "Why are you talking such nonsense? What is coming over?"

I never said to her that I see things and that Spirit would tell me things. We separated a year later. The night I was leaving home I said, "When I leave they will come and dig a big hole in front of the house and they will bury you." Now I know its not a nice thing to say but I saw it in a glance, but it was meant to be a joke. I left the night of the May 7, 1977 and the next morning they were actually digging a big hole. The City came to repair a pipe. She was frightened and came to look for me to tell me what was taking place.

I said, "Well I saw it the night before."

Then she kind of believed what I was saying.

When my wife was pregnant we traveled to Niagara Falls. On our way back home from Toronto to Montreal on highway 401, I saw a vision of a man crossing the road riding a bike.

I said to her, "Did you see the vision in front of you. Do you see anybody out there?"

She said, "No, I don't see anybody."

I said, "I see somebody" so I started to slow the car down. I released the gas and five minutes afterward there was a man, a drunken man riding a bike. I missed him by a few inches.

A few months after my divorce, Spirit would come to me and I would have visions. It was like a movie. And I had a hard time dealing with it.

So eventually I called my Mon and I said, "Mom, what can I do for it?"

She said, "Well there's two things. With your troubles I could send you money and you could come back home, or she said you could stay, face your problems and make yourself a better man.

And she said to me, "If you leave, one day your kids would say that you left them. If you stay and work and take care of your kids and support them they will look at you with respect. She said, "One is a short fix and one is a long fix. But she says do this for me. She said pray and I'll pray with you. She said pray in a special way. It's a good prayer"

Very often my mother and my family would pray in a special way.

All right she said, "There's a prayer for anything in life you need to accomplish. And she says, three days after you will see a monk crossing the boulevard. She said, do not kill him but stop and ask him to pray for you."

So I said, "OK" and I hung up the phone.

THREE DAYS LATER

Three days later I was going down the Boulevard Dorchester in Montreal and who is crossing the street but a monk. I hit the brake and he looked around.

He says, "Are you OK?"

I said, "Yes." I said, "Could you stop a minute, so he stopped. I pulled along side and I said, "My mother said that you should pray for me."

He said, 'I will pray for you but who is your mother?"

So I told him who my mother was.

He said, "I don't know your mother."

I said "No".

So he said, "Where is your mother?"

I told him that she was almost 5000-7000 miles away.

And he looked at me and he says, "She told you that I have to pray for you?"

And I said, "Yes"

So he stopped for a moment and smiled. He was a Franciscan monk and he says, "Well if you come back in an hour I will talk to you for a few minutes if you want."

I said, "That will be very nice of you. I said. Where?"

And he says, "Right across the street."

I crossed that boulevard for many years and I never realized there was a monastery there. So I said, "I'll be there in an hour's time."

So in an hour's time I went back.

And he said, "Let me get this thing straight. Your mother told you that I have to pray for you and your mother doesn't live here she lives in Trinidad?"

I said, "Yes" So I told him a little bit about my family, then he laughed.

He says, "That's not strange at all. He says we have monks here who see Spirit and he says we don't tell everybody that. He says yes there are Spirits."

So he became my friend and I found a monastery to go to pray in a special way. And there was a particular monk that would do this once a year and he would pray for all the brothers and friars that passed away. When they died they were buried in the crypt below the church. When he prayed you would see all the friendly Spirits come out and pray with him. Not many people in the church would see Spirits. Those who did would come to me and we would discuss it. Sometimes we could tell they were mad and they would giggle. One monk in particular always smiled when we told him that.

He says, "Of course Jim there are Spirits. Some move on some don't and some stay around to help." He also told me that if we trust in Spirits they help us and guide us.

HOW MY CAR WAS MADE NEW AGAIN-SPIRIT DOES IT

I will go back to the days when I was much younger and the elders took me out to fish at night. So we left land. There was no sight of land, no sight of light. It was a clear blue night.

We fished for several hours and when it was time to go home they said, "OK take us home."

I said, "I don't know which way is home."

They looked at me and said, "Trust in your Spirit Guide. He says, look at the stars and which star you think will take you home then follow that star."

And so that is what I did. I chose a star to the northern side. After an hour or two, I started to see light and then I was on the way home.

So they looked at me and said, "Did you learn a lesson? Let the Spirit guide you"

They said, "Sometimes Spirit guides you and sometimes they leave you to guide yourself. They said, they are good and they are bad. Sometimes when you think that something happens drastically, if you trust in Spirit, Spirit will make it turn out favorably when you least expect it."

As the old saying goes, 'when you pray you always get what you want' but it comes in a different way.

For instance, I had a car that I bought brand new and it was getting on in years. One morning I left home going to the office and I looked at the car and I said, "You know Doris If I had money, I would fix you up like brand new and I grabbed that thought and I threw it back into the Universe and asked for help from Spirit.

Going back to my car, as I continued up on Cote St. Ann I saw this lady coming and there were two Stop Signs on her side. She did not stop so I gunned the car to get away from her. In doing so she still hit me on the side. So we stopped and exchanged information of insurance and stuff like that and out of her purse came a picture of Mother Provential Help.

I looked down at it and right away in my mind I said, 'thank you Blessed Mother' thank you.

I looked at the lady and I said, "First, do you pray to her?" And I said, "I do pray to her too." And before that happened she was hysterical because of the accident so I tried to calm her down a couple of times. Finally we exchanged information.

And I said, "Did you see the sign?"

And she says, "Well I had so much on my mind I saw you coming and yes you were trying to get away from me."

I said, "Yes I know."

And she says, "Well I was on my way to the hairdressers because my daughter is getting married today.

I said, "Oh I said well jump into my car. I think we can still go. I'll drop you at the hairdresser. So I said, when you get there, have a hot cup of coffee to relax yourself. I said, "It's only a car. Have your hair done and have a good wedding."

She says, "How can I when all this happened?"

I said, "Nothing happens without a purpose and so its true."

When I went to the office afterward, her husband called and he said to me, "My wife really creamed you."

And I said, "She did cream me."

He said, "Son, go to your garage and have it repaired. Let me know how much."

So I said, "OK" and I took it to my garage.

I said, "Tendal, how much would you charge me to bring this car up to brand new? "

He says, " What happened?"

I said, "Somebody broke the Stop Sign and hit me"

He said: "OK here's the estimate. Send it to the person.

So I called him back and told him how much it was going to cost.

He says, "Fix it and fix it like new. "

I said, "Thank you" and within two days the check was in the mail but the car had not been repaired completely yet.

Tendal says, "Do you know this gentleman?"

I said, "No but I think he came in Spirit."

So he looked at me and laughed and says, "Yes."

So this was one of my encounters with Spirit. And I had my car like new and I said, "Thank you Spirit for that."

MY SECOND OPERATION

Now all my family is Catholic and we are mystical Catholics because of our beliefs. We do believe in the Virgin Mary. We do believe in Jesus. We do believe in God and very often I will pray to the Blessed Lady. Actually I've seen her appear before me a few times.

She appeared before me the first time I went in the hospital to repair my hernia. Now I am back in the hospital for a second operation on that same hernia. When I went into the operating room I heard about cases where people were awake while the operation was going on.

While I was on the operating table I said to the nurse, "You know nurse, my IV is out of my hand," but before I said that I saw the Blessed Mother in front of me and I was talking to her.

And she said, "Tell the doctor to repair it properly this time"

And I did tell the doctor.

And the doctor says, "Jim you should be asleep."

So then I tell the nurse, "Please check, my IV is out."

She says, "That's impossible but when she came around she saw yes it's true.

She put the IV back in and I said, "Oh, you are a Phillipino. She says, "How do you know that?"

I told her what island she was from in the Phillipines.

And she says, "How in the hell do you know that?"

I told her the size of the needle in my hand. It was a 22 gauge.

She says, "How do you know that? She was getting upset.

I drifted back out and the Blessed Lady disappeared.

While I was in recovery the same Phillipino nurse came to me. I was still half in and half out and I said, "I'm OK. I'm coming out of it."

She said, "How in the hell do I know? I'm looking at you."

I say, "I can see that."

And she says, "You're strange."

And I said, "Yeah, thank you."

I HAD A DREAM

Very often when I go to sleep I have dreams Spiritual dreams. A Spiritual dream is where I believe I was asleep but I was not asleep. I'll tell you about an encounter. One night around 3:00 am, I got up from sleep and I started to see beautiful butterflies, especially the Monarch butterfly and they were going south from Canada to a special place in Mexico. In my dream-sleep, I called it the Sierra del Madre the Chabas.

I would see all the butterflies in the snow and they were all dying and dropping from the trees and I said, "This is a strange Spiritual encounter."

In the morning I got up and I went to work. I crossed the street to a Mexican restaurant and saw my Mexican friend and I said, "Do you know a place called Chabas?"

He said, "Yes I know Chabas. He said, "Why?"

And I told him what took place.

He says, "Ah you are a Calendaro?"

I said, " Well, maybe, I'm not for sure."

But he says, "But ah, what you said is very true but I've never been to that part of Mexico yet in my life.

And he was amazed and says, "Sometimes things happen like that to people. He said, "You are a very special person."

MY WONDERFUL SON AND DAUGHTER

Well as you know I have a beautiful daughter and she got her first boyfriend. His name was John.

It's around Christmas time and my daughter says, "Dad you are invited for supper."

And I said, "Thank you.

She said, "Mom wants you to come for supper even though we were divorced then."

I went to supper and my daughter showed me what she bought for her boyfriend, whom she met six months ago.

And I looked at her and I said, "Stacy, do not give it to him."

She looked at me and she says, " Dad and why not give it to him?"

I looked at her and said, "In three days time he is going to leave you."

She says, "How could you say that? Dad I love him."

I said, "Yes I know you love him but I love you too and it will be a waste of money."

So she followed my advice. Dinner came and everything was fine.

The day after her boyfriend John came to her and he says, "Stacy, I want to tell you something"

So my daughter said to him, "Its OK and I know what you want to tell me"

So he says, "How could you know what I'm going to tell you? I haven't told you."

She says, "Well my Dad told me" and she told him exactly what he was going to do. So he was amazed. And she said, Oh there's one thing I can tell you about my Dad, he's a very special person."

On the same subject I am going to tell you an incident with my son who is a couple of years younger than my daughter. He was seeing a young lady and she broke his heart. To make a long story short, she left him for his friend and he was devastated and he wanted to take his life. One night I saw that and the time had come when he was going to do that.

My ex called me and she said, "Please I need help. Tommy called me from a phone booth somewhere in the city. I don't know where it is and we can't trace the call"

So I called one of my friends that I knew and she says, "Let's put our heads together and I'll guide you through this. She described everything and where he was going to be. I went down the street exactly where she told me and with my intuition I was guided to the correct place and found my son in the phone booth on the ground. The phone was hanging off the hook.

And that's one of my stories too. It had a happy outcome.

I told Tommy, "Sometimes life does not have good things for people but we all have to endure it, for things do turn around."

A SPECIAL FRIEND

I started working for a company in 1971. I got a call from the office for a meeting. They called and told me to deliver a bottle of shampoo. A bottle of shampoo is only $2.75 and I drive a big car so how much money could I make for $2.75. But again, I am trusting in Spirit Guides. They told me to take the call. So I went on the call and rang the bell and this gentleman came out with a cigar in his mouth and he spoke in French.

And I said, "Yes, well you ordered the shampoo?"
And he says, "Yes." I saw his wife in the back in the kitchen.
She said, "Let him in. This guy is a very special person."
When I walked into the house, I felt a little uncomfortable.
She came out of the kitchen she looked at me and she says, "What's wrong with your ear?
I said, "My ear, nothing is wrong with my ear."
And she says, "Yes, something is wrong with your ear"
I says, "No"
She says, "I saw you this morning jumping with your ear"
I said, "Oh my God I said I was washing my ear with shampoo and water from the shower got into my ear and I was trying to get it out"
She says, "I saw that"
And I said to her," I hope you like what you saw"
She says, "Oh God, if I was 25 years younger I would marry you."
And then my face turned red. I looked at her and said, "This lady is a very special lady," and I told her.

And she says, "You also are very special and she said come back to me one day and I'll explain."

I said, "You know I believe in God."

She says, "Me too."

I said, "I pray to the Blessed Virgin"

And she says, "Me too." And she says, come back in few days and I'll explain it to you."

So I did go back in few days and we sat and she started to explain things to me. And that was the first time in my life that I was receiving knowledge that was from somebody who knew knowledge. She told me that she was a nun before and she left the convent and got married. So I remained friends for a long time with this lady who gave me a reading and gave me guidance. She also coaxed me into developing what I had. So I kept in touch with her and still do today.

MY MOM PASSED AWAY AND IS IN SPIRIT

As I was walking down the street and I met a group of people. There were three of them and this lady was in the middle.

When I looked at her and she came directly toward me and she says, "You work across the street?"

I said, "Sure I do."

She says, "I have a friend working across there too." And she was talking and said, "I love ice cream just as you do." And she said, you are a very special person. "

So I looked at her intrigued and I said, "What do you do?"

And she told me that she also is clairvoyant. And she says, "You are a clairvoyant. Come to me and I'll teach you because I do teach it too.

I said, "OK I will come and see you" I went to see her and she taught me things that I knew in a way but I didn't know how to put them together and she told me to see Sara. I kept on keeping company with her, but she eventually passed.

One Sunday morning in 1985, I got up around 6:00 am. I went to my window and put on the kettle.

Like everything else, animals tell us things, and birds tell us things. This little birdie came to my window and when it came to my window I knew it was not bearing good news and I said to myself, 'Oh no, no, no not today.' And the bird flew away again. I called my friend and I said, "Is your Mom and Dad OK?

She says, "Yes" and she is getting a little bit scared.

So I invited her to have dinner with me. And she did come.

Around 7:00 pm my daughter called and said, "Are you sitting or are you standing?"

So I said to her, "Stacy when you finish with me I'll be sitting on the floor crying."

She said, "They've been trying to get hold of you all day. How do you know what I told you?"

I said, "I knew this morning."

She says, "Who told you?"

I told her that the bird came to me.

And she says, "Dad, you couldn't do anything?"

I said, "Not when it comes to that." You know the funniest thing sometimes I see things, and they help me to cope with it.

I didn't have enough money to travel home so I called upon Spirit, and said, 'I trust in you and if I have to go I will go.' In three days everything fell into place. The strangest thing is that I got onto the plane in a different city and a sister whom I hadn't seen in quite a while got on the same plane with me. We were flying home to bury my Mom. We stopped over in Barbados. I got off the plane to stretch my legs and I saw one of my friends in Spirit getting married in Barbados. And I said to myself. 'I must keep it and tell her.'

In our tradition when one passes away, we pray for nine days. Every night they would pray and I would not join them. Instead, I would be on the balcony looking at the stars and meditating and talking with my Spirit Guide. On the ninth day a large butterfly came from nowhere and hovered over me. A funny sensation, the hair on my head raised and for some reason

I knew it was the Spirit of my Mom. She flew into the room and hovered over everyone who was praying. I went into the room where she was staying and something told me to go after the butterfly and set it free. Everybody looked at me as I crossed into the room and tried to hold the butterfly but I couldn't. I said, "Mom, is that's you?" I pointed towards the door. The butterfly hovered over me and then went out into the night. Now the next day was Sunday and I went to the old church. There is an old, Irish, Benedictine priest there.

After mass was finished I went to him and said, "Father could you tell me something?"

And he says, "What did you see?"

So I confused him. He asked me what it is I saw? What did I want? So I told him about the butterfly.

He says, "That's the Spirit of your Mom. There are some things you can look for, like a feather. If the feather is white it is much better than if it is gray. And if it's a butterfly, the bigger the butterfly the better it is."

And I said, "Thank you Father." Somehow I got some knowledge from him.

I returned to Canada and I went to the monastery very close to my office where there are three monks. One of them is named Banfield. He knows me and when I asked for him he comes out.

He said, "I'm very sorry about your loss. I saw the butterfly too." And before I started telling him anything he started telling me what took place

And I said to him, "You can see it too?"

He says, "Of course we do" He said, just pray to your Mom and she will be with you any time you want in your life."

And I told him it was an amazing thing for him to say.

MY FRIEND IS NOW IN SPIRIT

After that I found myself a nice girlfriend. One evening close to Halloween, she came by and she says, "I'm going to bake for you, a nice pumpkin pie because I know you like pumpkin pies." That morning she left and went to the university to her class and in the evening she came back. When I came back in the room she was not there. A while later she arrived. I also told her when I met her that I'm a strange person, well not very strange but I see things and when she came to kiss me I knew that she had been unfaithful that day. So I told her about it and she was very astonished. I left and I went to the Children's hospital, for what reason I don't know. I guess this is what Spirit directed me to do. I spent about two hours in the hospital then I came home and the next day she was gone. She called me a while later and we became good friends.

I rented an apartment and became friends with my upstairs neighbor. She invited me up to have coffee with her. One day in particular as I walked by her bathroom I stopped and I looked at her.

She knew the kind of person I was and that I see things and I said, "Be careful when you go to take a bath because I see you drowning in the bathtub, lying in the bathtub" After a year and half the drowning happened. She was epileptic and hid it from everybody. She had an epileptic seizure in the bathtub and she passed away.

I had a strange thought to find how she was. For the next few days, I tried to find her. I knew that it was Sunday when she had drowned. I saw it on Saturday. She had invited me up for coffee. On Monday morning the dogs came to the tree in front of me and they were barking, and I knew then it was confirmed that she had passed away. I put it off. On Wednesday morning I got up and went upstairs. I asked the other neighbor to come with me. She had passed away in the bathtub. The police came and the ambulance came and the police treated me like a suspect. So I went to the police station. They took my statement. Then I had to go back again to give another statement. The second time when I returned, Spirit told me to tell them exactly what I am and how I am. There were two detectives and three policemen there.

I wrote the same statement and then I said to them, "I am one of eight kids. My daughter works for the government. I said, "I've been working for my company since 1971. I am a manager and I am a member of the Center." It was only then that they told me that the case was closed.

And when they were finished they looked at me and they said, "Did you know how she passed away?" I said, "I have an idea." And I never heard from them again. I still miss my neighbor and my friend. I still pray for her and I send her into the Light.

HOW I CAME TO BE HERE AT THE CENTER

I'll start with my doctor now. His office was at the Center on St Andrews Street. I go to the Center to have a check up when I have a cold. And there was a magazine there. When I opened the magazine a lady's name appeared, the famous Susan Trossler. I looked at the magazine and I looked at a boy I knew and

I said, " One day I will see this lady."

He said, "She comes here once in a Blue Moon."

I said, "Yes." So every time she came I missed her. I did not go there often, so fate didn't bring me to see her. So I told my friends, I said, "Look, one day I'll see her. One day she's going to ring me."

And they said, "Oh yes, right."

Three years went by and in 1975 one the secretaries from the Center was there. On that day I came to pick up my friend. Susan Trossler was outside and my friend introduced me to her.

And she said, "This is my friend Jim."

So Susan says, "Give me and hug."

And I give her a hug.

And my friend says, "No one here gives people a hug." When Susan Trossler hugged me she said, "This guy has to come to the Center. We need him at the Center."

So my friend looked at me and she says, "OK" So she got in the car she says, "What's so good about you that she had to say that?"

So I kind of smiled at her.

The next day I asked Susan Trossler to give me a reading.

I called and she said, "Sure you can have a reading with me." I called and that afternoon Susan gave me a reading. Amazingly enough when she finished I said, "How much do I owe you?"

She says, "Nothing, just come to the Center. My friend who was with me was amazed. And this is how I started with the Center. I have many encounters with Spirit at the Center. Today I am clairvoyant at the Center. I'm a medium at the Center. I have many more encounters with Spirit at the Center.

THREE NEAR COLLISIONS-HOW SPIRIT GUIDES ME

I told my niece in Toranto what I was doing at the Center and she was happy for me.

Christmas time was coming around and she says, "Well come down to Toranto for Christmas" I did go and stayed for Chistmas with them. I hadn't spent Christmas with them for quite a while. On Boxing Day we went to Downtown Toronto to see her friend who was from Scarborough. On the way back highway 401 was busy so I took the Old Kingston Road and it started to snow.

It was taking a long time coming back home and I saw in my rear view mirror on my right side this van was coming and I said to them, "This van is going to be in trouble." As soon as the van passed me I released my foot from the accelerator and started to slow down. As it was set and done like that, this van started to skid in front of me skidded from one end to the other and ended up in a church yard. I did not stop because I knew he was safe.

And I told my niece and her husband, "I'm sure this guy is going to church tomorrow morning. Already he's at church."

Then my niece said, "Uncle, you saw that before?"

She said, "I saw it only after they started skidding. I believed what you said."

I said, "You'd be amazed what I see sometimes."

Life is full with good things through meditation. I know that you can also see Spirit through meditation. Learning how to meditate is very good for people. It is also good for your health. My eating habits have changed drastically. I no longer drink and I eat less red meat and chicken. I'm not a complete vegetarian but I'm getting to like the food. My life is dedicated to Spirit and good things happen very often.

I'm going back say 6 years ago on a Friday morning.

My neighbor upstairs was leaving to go up North and somehow I was looking at her truth and I said, "You know, I should drive her up North because I knew and sensed the feeling that she would have an accident to put it bluntly." So then she left and I didn't bother talking to her of anything like that. On a Sunday night to be exact when she was on her way home she passed out on the highway. That's in the mountains. She went from one side of the road to the other side and the car flipped three times. I guess the Angels were with her because she survived it with only a few bruises and was hospitalized up North, but her car was a total wreck. In the morning, before 10:00 am, the phone rang and it was her asking if I could pick her up to bring her back home because she had nobody to help her at that time.

As I dropped everything to go up North to pick her up, I told myself, 'You know what, I've seen all this before but didn't remember it.' So when I got to the hospital I was bringing her back down and told her what I saw.

As she says, "You know something, if you would have told me that before I would not have ventured up North"

But I said to her, "Sometimes things are better left undone or unsaid." In a way I guess it was meant to be that way.

Going back another two years this is another story of mine. It was an evening during the week and I went to bed say around 10:30 pm and I fell asleep. Around 1:00 am in the morning I started to have what I call a sleep but not a sleep. I see things also when I dream and sometimes I'm half asleep but sound asleep. And there were three young men and I realized very vividly in the dream that it was my friend's sons and they were coming back from Ottowa and it was snowing and the car went off the road. Somehow in my state of mind I was in the car with them driving the car to bring it out of the spin. They came out of that accident without any danger or hurt. Actually they did pull the car out of the ditch and continued on their journey back.

MY TRIP TO TORANTO-SPIRIT TOOK OVER

After my Mom had passed away I became the manager of my company and I hired a lady from Trinidad.

After a few days on the job she looked at me and she says, "There's something about you that I can't pinpoint but by the end of the week it will come to me."

So I looked at her and smiled.

Before the end of the week she came to me and says, "You know, you are a very special person, very mystical person. And she said, "Well you know I was living in Toranto. I just came from Toranto."

I said, "Yes,"

She says, "I have a friend who lives in Toranto who is special like you."

I looked at her and I said, "Do you know your friend's name?"

And she told me her name was Martha.

So I said: "One day you will take me to see Martha."

And she said, "I don't see how that's possible because I'm now living in Montreal.

I said: "Just put that thought back into the Universe. She then moved to another office. One day she called me in a panic, that she had to go to Toronto on an emergency and she had nobody to take her there. Her son in the family stilled lived there.

So I said, "OK I will do so." The next day we left for Toranto.

Half way on our way to Toranto she says, "You know I made an appointment with my friend Martha and I didn't realize that you were going to be taking me."

I said, "Don't worry about it because they are expecting two people."

She says, "Is she?"

I said, "Yes when we get there they will tell you that she was expecting two people."

She says, "Wait a minute here. Didn't you tell me this a few years ago?"

I said, "Yes I did." And she giggled.

THE LOTTERY

Now let me tell you about a classic one here. I have a friend, a long time friend who played music with me and there's a funny twist to it. One day my eldest brother and his mother, my oldest brother's wife and his mother are first cousins and I never knew that for a long time but I knew somehow we were connected and we used to travel together.

One day I looked at him and I said to him, "You know we play the lottery and one day one of us is going to win pretty big." So that time it was his time. He won the two million bucks. But many times before that I saw that he was going to win big. We had a strong bond because of the family ties with my brother.

A FRIEND, FLOWERS AND PRAYER

Now coming back to my friend with her three sons. The first time I met her she was a manager in one of the boutiques close to my office. She brought in a unit to be repaired. The unit was repaired and she took it with her. She used it and she wasn't too happy about its performance. She took it back to the office and blasted off at everybody. They wanted to charge her for another part. She was not happy about that. So I saw her and something connected with me. She left and went back to the boutique. I left the office and paid her a visit. I went in and apologized for what was happening to the machine. She was very upset.

I looked at her and she was blasting everything off and I said, " I see you in a yellow dress planting flowers in the garden."

And she stopped and looked at me. She says, "How do you know I love gardens?"

I said, "Well this is what I see."

So then her whole tone and attitude changed right away. And she says, "Is there something you want to tell me?"

I said, "Yes, one day you are picking flowers and giving them to me because I'm paying you a visit."

And she looked at me and she said, "You paying me a visit?"

I said, "Yes."

So to make a long story short when the day that happened, she was down in the flower garden in a yellow dress.

And she said, "Goodness, I'm in a yellow dress. I'm in the garden and here you are in front of me and how is it I'm offering you flowers?"

I said, "Doesn't that ring a bell?"

She says, "Yes, it does. You told me that three years ago."

And I said, "The flowers that you are giving me are for the Blessed Lady.

And she says, "What do you mean, Blessed Lady?"

I said, "Because I go in the mountains and there is a beautiful statue of the Blessed Lady that I take flowers to."

And she says, "I didn't know that."

Now there is a part of me that not many people know. I am spiritual, I am mystical but I am also Catholic by faith and I also pray. I pray in a special way and one of my ventures is to go to the Blessed Lady to pray. There's a little thing that happens very often when I go to pray. When I go to St. Patrick's Cathedral in the city I kneel before the statue of the Blessed Lady, actually she is called the Mother of Perpetual Help. After a few minutes, when I look at the icon, the icon turns into three dimensions. I can see that she's really in dimension like 3D. Then I pray and when anyone who comes and kneels along next to me, I pick up whatever they have come to pray for. But there is a thing about that. As much as I would like to tell them the good side of what is happening to them I cannot because I was told not to by the Center. So, that's another thing. But I keep praying for people.

I NEEDED MONEY-SPIRIT PROVIDED IT

Turning on another subject, a few years ago, I needed a bit of money and the day before I was telling myself, 'I can do with a few thousand dollars' and I threw it into the Universe. The next day I was going up a certain street, it was up a hill like and what I saw in front of me was a night bag. So I stopped and picked it up and looked inside. There were no names, no checks, no credit cards, no receipts, nothing at all but a few thousand dollars and when I say thousand I mean a few thousand dollars. I took it up and waited and see or hear if anybody dropped it. I waited for a while and nobody was on the news or in an ad. Nobody claimed it and you know where it went? I dropped the empty night bag into the post box. I don't know where it went to from there but I said thanks to Spirit. That's another one of my things. When I do need money, I send the thought into the Universe and somehow it comes and I always thank Spirit for it.

MY ASTRAL DREAMS

About three years ago I got up in the middle of the night, around 3:00 am and I was in an astral dream. First I saw myself in a beautiful little cottage in the mountains. It was at night the moon was bright and the stars were shinning. I met a young gentleman who came to look for me. I can't remember his name.

He was asking me if I had certain powers and I said, "Son you've come to the right place at the right moment and with that a glow came over me, a light shined down on me and I began to raise my hand and I elevated my body.

He was so amazed that he was in fright but I said, " Do not be frightened. It's only me here to show you what Spirit can do. When I was finished and came back down, a comet shot across the sky and the young man was quite amazed. And this is one of my journeys of my spiritual side of life.

A few months ago again I got up one morning in the middle of dream/sleep. I am in a café here in Canada among friends. I ordered café o laity and several orders of café o laity for my friends who were with me. They also wanted to drink café o laity. They drank it from a bowl. Actually my bowl dropped from my hand and as it dropped I concentrated on the fall of the bowl and the bowl began to spin very fast and the coffee, instead of falling out onto the ground swiveled like a tornado and went right back into the bowl. Everybody around me was amazed. These are recollections of my spiritual experiences and what I do once in a while.

Well here we are again. Last night I got up around 4:00 am drank a little bit of milk and went back to sleep and immediately I had an astral dream. I'm traveling and I meet this beautiful lady.

She says, "Son, here is a gift for you."

And it was a big bag, a paper bag, gift bag with crepe paper and beautiful design on the bag. So I looked at her and turned around I says, "Thank you very much, thank you for the gift and I gave her a hug and I said to myself, 'Well, someone finally gave a gift.' I don't usually get gifts from strangers but here it was.

She left and something told me to look and see what the gift was. I opened the bag, removed the paper and it was a spider, a very odd spider. It wasn't a black spider. It wasn't a white spider either. It was not a tarantula. So I put the spider back in the bag. In my culture we are taught to respect spiders. There is saying, if a spider comes in the morning it means sorrow, at lunchtime it means borrow and in the evening is money and joy.

So she says, "Nurture him, feed him, and take care of him."

I continued my journey and I ended up in a shopping center and in a restaurant. In this vision everybody is feeding me and I didn't have to pay for it.

And I said, "What is going on?" Anyway I looked around and I looked for my spider and it was gone. It was missing. I got up to look for the spider. A lot of people in the restaurant were helping me look for the spider. We found the spider. The spider she gave me was a female but the spider we found was a male, so I picked both of them up and put them in the bag. I finished my dinner and then went home. To my surprise and amazement, the next morning I found lots of baby spiders.

I said to myself, 'Oh they have copulated and I have a whole family.' I put all the spiders back into the bag and continued on my journey. But here is the thing. I went through all my books and all my visions and they say spider is money.

I've seen Spirit. One night I woke up around 2:30 am. I fell back asleep but I was in twilight and I was in a different place on the earth and time. In the distance, before me were giants, native giants of different colors, but all native guides and I approached them. They were very friendly and they asked me who my Guide was. When I stood next to them I spoke a language that I didn't know, that I never heard before and they spoke a language that I never heard before either but still we communicated. And when I stood next to them they were almost twice my size in height and there were six of them. So I enjoyed the time I spent with them.
    They said, "Goodbye." I hugged them and they hugged me and we went on our merry way.

As I continue my Astral journey into the Spirit world, one morning I got up out of bed and found myself in a gathering of people, strange people that I did not know.
    They looked at me and said, "I came to collect an inheritance.
    As I approached them I said, " I don't know."
    One looked at me and said, "You are just on time. You are the true one"
    I looked at everyone and said, "Who are you?"
    And they said, "That does not matter." The inheritance was from a person who had passed away and left an inheritance for me. And they said, "You are just on time for it"

I turned around, they gave me the letter and everybody was gone and to my astonishment I was back in the room. So I took it as a very spiritual event.

As I continue my journey I see things happen. Here is another short event. One morning I woke up at 3:00 am. In my astral dream there was a beautiful lady but she only had one eye. She was blonde. The eye was blue, deep blue and she talked to me. She told me many things about my spiritual journey. As I looked at her carefully she changes again but this time she had two eyes instead of one.
And I said to her, "How come you have two eyes but before you had only one?"
She says, " I am in the realm of Spirit. So that is why you see me this way."
And I says, "May I go back to sleep?"
She says, "Yes,"
As I lie down to close my eyes a bright light came over me and I said, 'Thank you Spirit wherever you came from." And then the light disappeared. I thought I had turned the lights off in my place but then I looked around and went back, there was light again. Finally after a few seconds the light disappeared.
This is a story that one night my Spirit Guides came to me. They appeared before me with painted faces and masks across their faces. But here is the thing. They were all women, women Spirit Guides. Sometimes it's unusual but not all that unusual. Then they were pointing me to something like a Cathedral a very old Spiritual Church, with a lot of candles all lit, all white candles and they were telling me I have to go light some candles. And the candles were there for the Spirits. After I had done that I was in the church with them and they continued on the journey with me. We ended up in a Chocolate Store looking at

chocolates and the price of chocolates. There was a big pack of chocolates for $35.00 and a small pack for $8.00. I'm still trying to put together what the numbers 35 and 8 mean but usually it's a good spiritual dream. Were my Spiritual Guides telling me that they needed chocolate? This is sometimes how they appear and how I see them. And I leave you with this story.

I continue another journey a few weeks before. My mother came to me. My mother was in Spirit and she came to invite me for dinner. She was dressed in red- hot shoes and looked then about 40 years old. She took me to a restaurant, not a very posh one, but not a greasy spoon either. We enjoyed the food and we spent time together.
When we finished, she got up and she said, "It's my treat"
I offered to pay for the food. I said, "Mom I have money.
"No need to pay." She says, I insist that I want to pay. With that she took some money out of her purse and said, "Here son, go pay for the food for the dinner."
So then I realized it was foreign money. It was not the money of the land. So I took it and said to myself 'It's a good thing I have money to pay for the food.' So I paid for the food but I kept the money that she gave me and then I gave it back to her.
I said, "We cannot pay with this money."
She says, "Keep it. I'm giving it to you."
The dream here is very symbolic. My Mom gave me a windfall from the Spiritual world and I thank her very much for that.

As I continue my journey, I am traveling in Spirit with people I didn't know. I find myself in a foreign land. There were giant castles. I entered a castle and I looked at the concrete walls how thick they were. Inside the castle was a Casaba, and big Casaba Circle looking out and I was admiring the structure.

Then I moved on from there and went toward the sea. There was a new development of homes; beautiful homes and I said to myself, 'I never knew these things existed in these parts.' And I was admiring them. I went into one home and there were a lot of people around. Then I continued on the path and it went to the sea. Oh what a beautiful place.

There was a slip for boats, ships and the sea was calm. There were a lot of activities and I said to myself, 'I would love to live here it's a beautiful place. It's by the ocean, with fresh air and a nice breeze.' And this is one of my spiritual journeys too.

THAT BUS NEARLY HIT ME

This is a short story, actually a true one. Yesterday morning, and the night before were very cold. We had blinding snow but still it was sunny. It's winter and we are in February. As I turned a corner to enter a street, Spirit kicked in, and told me to slow down. A car came up behind me and the driver was tooting his horn to drive faster. So I looked in my rear view mirror and made a sign for him to slow down but he took no heed. He began to toot again. So as I came to the corner I pulled aside to the right and he came in the middle lane, not knowing that I knew it was dangerous in back of him.

He could not stop and the bus was coming down the street and somehow I said, 'Look if he gets hit he will hit me too.' And I just said, 'Spirit, let the bus go away from him' and the bus went from him. So sometimes Spirit guides us and tells us things to do and we have to take heed. So ego had stepped into this guy, and it nearly cost his life. The bus would have definitely creamed him and well I would have gotten hit too because I was on his right. We both were turning right in the cross street. It's good to listen to our Spirit Guides, when they tell us to do certain things. And I'll leave you with that. It's a short story.

Sometimes we have dreams about future events. It could take a month or even a year before they come true. Often we fail to link our dreams to reality. Only when the dream has taken place do we realize what the connection was. It's good to follow your instincts and your dreams. Sometimes dreams tell us the future. If we can decipher them, they could be helpful to us. Definitely, we should think about it. It's something to think about because dreams do have a place in our life and the things we do. Actually we all have dreams.

When we get up and put our feet on the floor, we don't know how the day it is going to turn out. But still we get up and we say Thank You God and we continue. Most of us, when we go to bed don't say thanks for the day. Sometimes it's good to say thanks for the day. 'Spirit, thanks for the day.' Actually we know Spirit is God Almighty. It's good to be thankful for the small gifts we receive and sometimes we receive big gifts.

HOW MY LANDLORD GOT POORER

Now here is a strange story. This is a real story, one of my experiences. A while back my landlord sent me a letter for an increase in rent of $15.00. I wrote him back a registered letter and I offered him $5.00. He did not go and pick up the registered letter so I wrote another registered letter reminding him. He did not go and pick up that one either. So I wrote a third letter and I went to the janitor who we call a concierge here and I made him sign it that he received it. So after a few months went by I met my landlord and he was not too happy with the $5.00 increase.

So he says, "We'll take it to the Reggie. We have a court that we call the Reggie with a moderator that sees about these things here. But this has to do with Spirit.

So I said, "OK." I put it into Spirit's hands and I said to Spirit, 'You deal with it and you see that justice has begun.'

A month later, I got a letter stating that I had to appear before a Rental Board on a certain date. I did go to the Court where a judgment will be passed. There was a woman judge, the landlord and I. The landlord presented his case before the judge. He asked for eviction with recuperation of the money with interest.

So the Judge watched me and looked at me and says to me, "Why didn't you reply to the landlord?"

I said, "Well Your Honor, I did so."

She looked down at me.

So I said to the Judge, "May I approach the bench?" And I handed her my papers and I said, "Here you are, Your Honor. I sent two registered letters to him. He did not pick them up. I went to a different Post Office and then let the janitor sign for them."

And she looked at him and she said to him, "Why didn't you pick up your registered letters?"

He said that he never got any notice.

And she said, "Now you have a notice that the janitor signed on your behalf." So she says, "Would you like to do something in good faith?"

So I said, "Yes" and I offered him two dollars more.

He says, "No, I cannot accept that"

So then I said, "Two dollars and that's final." So he refused it.

The Judge looked at him and she said to him, "Do you know that you can lose it all?" But he took no heed.

So I looked at the Judge and I said, "I'll leave it up to you. You be the judge. I trust you and I trust your judgment."

So she says, "May I keep your papers?"

And I said, "By all means do"

A month later, I got a letter in the mail with a judgment and guess what? I got a decrease of $100.00 instead of an increase of $5.00. So I meditated on this and put this thing in Spirit for almost three weeks and whatever judgment the Spirit gave I respected it.

Sometimes when we work with Spirit we can get things done. And I thanked Spirit for the judgment. So now here is the thing. He has to go back and contest it. It could be the same judgment that the Judge made or it could be a clerical error, but I say it's the judgment that Spirit makes. We shall see what the outcome is eventually. Putting faith in Spirit does work wonders.

THE LADY AND HER FEATHER

This is a story about the spiritual part of two people. One is a young lady 33 years old that comes from a different land and was to meet someone that she doesn't know for the first time. I was given the message in a dream a few days before she arrived. This lady lives in Spain. She was coming to stay with us a while to learn about knowledge and Spirit.

She arrived one night at the Center. I didn't know who she was. I was on the platform, the service platform.

I looked at her and I said to myself, 'She's from Spain and she has a message for me.' So after the service was finished, I approached her and I introduced myself and she introduces herself.

I looked at her and I said, "Tell me, do you have a very important question to ask me?"

And she blushed and she said in Spanish, "I am shy." I said, "No need to be shy. If there is something, you have a message for me by all means tell me. It would be of help to you.

She says, "Ok, three days before I came to this country, my father who is in Spirit showed me a man who is oriental looking. At first I thought he was Japanese. I thought he was Chinese, but he was oriental looking. My father said to me, "This man will take care of you if you have any problems or questions that you need to know about knowledge and he will finally tell you and guide you. He's here to guide you.

And she said to me, "I just realized that person is you and she said, "This is strange. Three days before I arrived my father was guiding me."

I said, "Well Spirit can teach you in mysterious ways."

She passed her time at the Center. I guided her along then one night I was on the platform again I looked at her and I said, "You know you sleep with a feather across your mouth sometimes."

She said, "Yes, I do. She said, "How do you know that?"

I said, "Well, Spirit just told me" and said, anytime you see this feather again, it's your father."

The next morning she got up and there was a white feather next to her bed and she was all excited and she came down and showed us the feather. She was amazed and did not know how the feather got there. So she took the feather to Reverend Sentel and he blessed the feather for her.

And I told her, "Always keep that feather in your possession. Anytime you want to see your father or talk to your father, sleep with the feather across your mouth."

Again this is sometimes the way Spirit works.

THE POWER CIRCLE

As I continue my Spiritual journey I have joined up with one of the teachers at the Center, His name is Peter Tamblis. This meditation takes place in the evening at 7:30 pm. I was invited to lead a Spiritual Power Circle meditation with Peter. Tonight, he will be officiating in the Circle and I will be participating in the Circle.

We prepare for the meditation. We have put incense, candles and a giant crystal in the Circle. We have blessed the room. We burned sage leaves. There were eight of us seated in the Circle. Reverend Tamblis takes us into meditation. He takes us into the Spirit World. I sit above everybody else because I'm the one who will bring messages tonight. As we go deeper into meditation, the wolves appear, a native wolf appears on my right side and then one on my left. And the wolves stay with us quite a while. One wolf moves from person to person as we continue our meditation. There are also bison that appear to us. We also see many things as we continue in the Circle. After we finished, we asked them what they saw in meditation and everybody saw the wolf. The wolf came and crossed over them. Then I described the wolf.

And they said, "Yes it was that color." When everybody joins in meditation, anything can appear in the Circle.

As we went back in again I began to elevate and shine. I can see the lights. I throw on the candle and I see the lights like the Aureole Borealis, the Northern Lights and the Northern lights came all over us as we sat into the Circle.

After we finished everybody opened their eyes and everybody said, "We saw lights, Northern Lights, the Aureole Borealis."

As we continued our meditation, we held hands and water came from the women's hands. They perspired water from their hands, only the women. The men were dry. And the women's hands became very cold as they sat there. They all had to warm up because they were very cold.

This is a Spiritual journey and what we do in a Power Circle, a Spiritual Circle.

A JOURNEY INTO THE RAIN FOREST

My niece passed away in 2007. She lived on the coast of Venezuela. One evening while I was in meditation in the Circle, her Spirit came into the meditation with me.

She came to me in Spirit form and she said, "Uncle, why not do a meditation on me and my journey into the Amazon."

So that came right into my head and I started the meditation on a journey into the Amazon. We had about 20 to 25 people and I've never had done this type of meditation before. I put myself in meditation mode and I saw her again.

And she says, "Uncle, let me guide you and this is how your meditation would start.

We start off in a little village on the Coast of South America in Venezuela called Carbito. Here we embark on a tour that will take us into the mouth of the Orinoco River, up into the Orinoco to the Amazon River. The Orinoco is one to the tributaries of the Amazon. As we embarked I guided everybody into the pirogue. The pirogue moved out from the large ship very smoothly and swiftly. We hit the coast of the South American Continent. We went south to the mouth of the Orinoco. A half hour later we see the mouth of the river. The mouth of the Orinoco is in the Atlantic, southern Atlantic. The water changes and the current changes. The water changes because you have a flow of fresh water and salt water mixing. As we begin this meditation we see the largest shrimps that you've ever see in your life, almost six inches long. We go up the Orinoco and have smooth sailing up the Orinoco. On the left side of the river, you see a beautiful glitter of gold and that glitter of gold is a small tamarind monkey. When the sun hits it, it shines like gold. And this is one of the world's wonders.

As you continue, right away there are three white dolphins. Real white dolphins are found only in fresh water, in one place in the world and that is the Amazon.

Indians also say they are spiritual creatures. They always welcome you when they come alongside the pirogue, to tell you that your journey will be safe. The Indians have already received word that we are coming. As you move further in, you see the giant cape bar. The sun beats down upon our faces, bringing us energy. The splash of the water is cooling us as you go and we imagine ourselves going back in time. Further ahead we see the Caymans. As you continue around the bend you see the giant macaw, beautiful scarlet ibis birds of paradise, and the humming bird. We see beautiful hibiscus flowers, rare ones, yellow, green, blue, purple and the bougainvilleas. You see the savannah along the river, the grass moves in waves with the gentle breeze.

But what I'm telling you in this mediation is actual reality. If you take a journey up there, this is actually what you will see. Now you continue and you see the giant Anaconda bending from the tree. There is no need to fear them because they are water reptiles. You see the turtles as they swim by. You see the school of piranhas as you continue your journey. Your journey is being protected and safe. In a few more minutes you turn the bend you and see the welcome party. Everybody is waiting to welcome your arrival but before that you pass villages of Indians who wave to you. The Mosquito Indians wave to us. As you enter the village of your destination, they are waiting on the banks to bring your boat onto land. As you disembark from the boat they all welcome you and put their hands around you. They give you a hibiscus flower to put in your hair and they lead you to the hut filled with fruits. You see the hammock, the children playing, and hear the sounds of the birds in beautiful harmony and imagine yourself in this time. On the left side you look and you see a beautiful waterfall. In the waterfall you see a pool, like a lagoon. You are being drawn to the waterfall. As you reach the waterfall you take your clothes off and you stay in your skivvies as you want to call it, and you go into the pool to refresh yourself.

And you say, "Oh, this water is so refreshing" In the air there is an aroma and you say, "What beautiful aroma is that?" As you spend a little more time in the pool you see the little fish as they swim by, the guppies. You look across to the other side and you see beautiful water lilies in bloom. The smell of the water lilies is incredible. Now as you approach the water lilies it's like a mat, but soon you realize it's a leaf and the leaves are like the shell of a giant pad. And you say to yourself, "Yes Lord, I have reached my destination of the giant lily pods." You get onto the giant lily pod and its keeps your weight up. It keeps you afloat. When you look into the water you see the giant tambaqui, the prize fish of the native Indians of South America. But here's the thing about these giant fish. They are fruit eaters and grass eaters. They will make a water spout and hit the fruit and the fruit will fall into the river, then they will go and eat it. After, they will pass the seeds whole into their stomachs. Yes there is a fish that eats grass and fruits and it's a prize fish. But as you sit on the giant lily pod and meditate you loose all track of time. And at this moment you tell yourself, "This is where you are supposed to be at this time and place in your life." You relax and take the energies from the lily pods and smell the aroma of the white and mauve flowers of these giant water lilies. Then you say, "How could this be real?" Only the creator can have such a thing. Yet everything I say that my niece took me in Spirit through this meditation is real. Think about it. I leave you and God bless.

Usually I play guitar in my meditation.

After the meditation was finished they turned around and said to me, "They never had a meditation like that before." Everybody was right there in the Amazon.

And I looked at them and said, "It is reality." And when you close your eyes you can travel anywhere you want even into the Amazon. If you go to the Amazon and go up the Orinoco into the village, the Indians, the Waorini Indians, you will see this reality and this reality does exist. But we have to leave our journey and come back down the river the same way that we went up. My niece's name is Meinda and she lives in Spirit now and I say Amen. As you notice I played some music to symbolize the words to help you can understand the meditation.

EPILOGUE

The curtain closes, the lights are dim once again. We've told out stories, Jim and me. We've told you what is in our hearts, from our deepest center where mind and body converge and meet the soul and perhaps in telling these stories you've had a glimpse of who we are. Our journeys continue as do yours and we pray you Godspeed and blessings and peace, joy, prosperity and most of all Love.

www.ingramcontent.com/pod-product-compliance
Lightning Source LLC
Chambersburg PA
CBHW070919180426
43192CB00038B/1947